Edited by Grace Keenan Prince

Diary Kid by John Patrick Teahan

Grace Prince Nov. 1999

Copyright © 1999 by Grace Keenan Prince

All rights reserved: no part of this book may be reproduced in any form or by any means, electronic or mechanical, except by a reviewer, who may quote brief passages in a review to be printed in a newspaper or magazine or broadcast on radio or television.

This book was published with the assistance of the Canada Council and others. We acknowledge the support of the Canada Council for the Arts and the Government of Canada through the Book Publishing Industry Development Program for our publishing activities. Canada

ISBN 0 7780 1115 1 (hardcover)
ISBN 0 7780 1117 8 (softcover)

Cover art by Mashel Teitelbaum
Book design by Michael Macklem

Printed in Canada

PUBLISHED IN CANADA BY OBERON PRESS

Contents

Training in England 13

Active Service with Canadian Forces 69

Officers' Training School 120

Officer with the Sherwood Foresters 134

On Sick Leave 171

On Leave in Canada & England 177

In France with the 16th Battalion 192

Preface

John Patrick Teahan was one of Canada's soldiers of the Great War who did not return home. Killed in action in 1916, Teahan was among the nation's 60,000 war dead.

But his legacy lives on in these splendid diaries, ably edited by his niece, Grace Keenan Prince. Secretly kept, the diaries constitute a remarkable document. Teahan's viewpoint is that of a soldier, and he is sharply observant, tough in judgment, compassionate in assessing the other ranks but less so when assessing officers. Teahan had the good fortune to rise from the ranks to a commission, but he remained more sympathetic to the ORs—and properly so. As his diary records, the officers he dealt with too often had more perks at their disposal than good judgment.

The diaries also provide a superb—if depressing—account of the First Contingent's training on Salisbury Plain in the dreadful winter of 1914-15, and they are excellent when describing life in the trenches and beyond the lines. As a cavalryman-turned-provost, Teahan had the duty and opportunity to move about. Military police are never much loved in any army, but we get the clear impression that Teahan was no bully with a club beating the men back into the trenches. Teahan also served (and died) with the "Imperials," and his account provides a Canadian eye on the ordinary British soldier that is refreshing in its directness.

These are splendid diaries, completely unknown until this publication, but certain ever after to have a secure place in the Canadian—and British—histories of the First World War.

J.L. GRANATSTEIN
Director and CEO, Canadian War Museum

Introduction

John Patrick Teahan was born in Southampton, Ontario in 1887, the eldest of twelve children. His father, Dennis, owned the Commercial Hotel there until 1906, when the family moved to Windsor where he opened a furniture store that John managed for him until the outbreak of the war.

He attended High School in Bradford, Pennsylvania and did a commercial course, including typing and shorthand. He was a Lieutenant in the Windsor Militia for some years prior to the war, and was the first man in the Windsor area to answer the call to colours at Amherst House, Amherstburg on August 14, 1914.

He was not married, nor did he leave a sweetheart behind, nor, indeed, (typically Irish—his seven brothers married late) did he seem to have any matrimonial plans in his immediate future for, in one entry, he expresses surprise at his comrades' intention to marry as soon as possible after the war. His future plans revolved around decorating the family home with war souvenirs: he was a keen collector, and shipped several packing-cases home from his travels in England and Europe.

Written in indelible pencil on small cheap newsprint booklets and smuggled out in various ways, the diaries have survived the intervening years concealed with family papers. John often reminded his mother (for they doubled as letters home) that they were to be kept very carefully and not passed about, as he put it, "like books in a lending library." All my life I have been hearing rumours of their existence, like a family myth, but they only came into my possession a few years ago and I was astounded at the detail and quality of the manuscripts.

The diaries, punctiliously numbered and dated, begin with his arrival in Plymouth, a 27-year-old corporal with the First Contingent (Royal Canadian Dragoons) in November of 1914 and end just prior to his death in Thiepval, France (by then he was a 2nd Lieutenant with the Sherwood Foresters Battalion, British Imperial Army) in October, 1916. Three books are missing—lost in the mail, and never accounted for. Their loss gave John considerable anxiety. He was very well aware of the punishment meted out to those who broke the rigid laws of censorship.

While leading his men through the "communication trenches" by which men and supplies were brought up to the front, John was wounded in March, 1916, near Fleurbaix and spent some time in military hospitals in France and England. He travelled home to Canada to spend a brief convalescent leave, and went back to light duties in England after which he returned to France.

It is the minutiae of his Service that he describes: training on Salisbury Plain; his duties with the Military Police; the tedium of the trenches (that is where he got his nickname of "The Diary Kid"), as well as the excitement of battle; sightseeing in London and France. He wrote under bombardment in dugouts and billets. He records drunkenness, incompetence, stupidity and waste and by degrees, his evolution from a keen (if green) warrior to a critical, cynical candidate for inglorious death in the mud. (He confided to a friend on his last leave that he knew he would not come back.) He does not dwell on the carnage—he deals with it elliptically. It is hard to interpret his reticence: either he did not care to dwell on the horrors for his own sake (he says in one entry from April 1915, "...it is impossible to write a clear description of anything like that, for me anyhow, and I simply overlook all lurid details") or he chose to spare his parents' sensibilities. Perhaps a little of both.

John Teahan was my uncle. To me, growing up in my grandmother's house, he was a sepia portrait of a grave, handsome soldier; three medals under glass and a formal letter of condolence from the King, hanging in a row in the front hall. I never heard her speak of him. No-one ever spoke of him.

A few anecdotes remain. My mother, Nora, then only nine years old, remembers his arrival, unannounced, at teatime in the summer of 1916. "Mother stood up, and walked straight to him in the doorway. She knocked over a large Chinese vase in her haste—and didn't even notice...."

He was a talented musician, and from an early age was in great demand as a singer at weddings and concerts throughout Southern Ontario. He was an amateur boxer, with something of a name in sporting circles. He was also interested in racing: his father used to take the boys to the big races, and a younger brother, Fred, ran away from home at sixteen to become a jockey, and a fairly successful one. The diaries are larded with sports slang and metaphor. He was, I gather, something of a ladies' man—though he spares his mother accounts of romantic exploits: on the return voyage to England, he confidently remarks that he bet his tablemates that he could steal a fellow officer's girl—and nobody would bet against him. (That passage was, for reasons of space, omitted from this book, but I offer it as another facet of his personality.)

His collection of guns and military equipment, pewter and china (sent from Europe in crates) was dispersed among his brothers. One shabby hand-sewn army pouch and a passenger list from the *Metagama*, which carried him back to England after a brief home leave, are preserved. That is all he left behind—except for these remarkable diaries which are more than an account of his war. They are the portrait of this soldier—reasonable, disciplined, sardonic, responsible, brave and compassionate; a bit of a prig, perhaps; a racist, certainly, but a man who could and did believe that the Supreme Sacrifice was worth the making.

GRACE KEENAN PRINCE

Editor's note: These journals (I have both photostats and a computer transcription of the originals, which are to be found in the National War Museum in Ottawa) have been reduced to a tenth of their original length. While I have, perforce, cut a great deal out, I have curbed the temptation to make improvements, such as rewriting the occasional grammatical mistake. John Teahan was a good speller but where he erred, I have not hesitated to correct him. Military men are devoted to dotting the i's and crossing the t's when it comes to their various battalions and divisions; I have cut this very specific data to the bone to make a smoother read. My uncle was also punctilious about such things as numbers and the time of day, which I have rounded off to move the story along.

Training in England

ARRIVAL AT PLYMOUTH

(Mailed from the Green Dragon Inn, Lavington Market, Wiltshire, where I came to get the first bath I have had since my arrival in England.)

November 15, 1914. Pond Farm Camp, Salisbury Plain. When we arrived off the coast of England on the *Laurentic*, everybody thought we were bound for Southampton, so we were surprised when the man-o'-war escorting the head of the procession swung around the Eddystone lighthouse toward the hills in the distance which Englishmen on board said was Plymouth. The secret of where we were eventually to land had been known only to the Officer in Command of the flagship and, possibly, he only received a wireless a few hours out of sight of England.

The soldiers, too excited to think about breakfast, were watching the torpedo boats and destroyers circling about. The fishing fleet was far out and coasting vessels were going by in the most peaceful way, as though they had never heard of the war.

About 9 a.m. we passed inside the long cement breakwater which is the centre of the outside harbour. There were forts on either side of the channel and also on an island in the basin. Plymouth looked like those cardboard towns you see in shop windows and all the fields were clear and distinct even at a distance. The fields were all colours, very square with hedges instead of fences and the wireless station looked like a toy. In the harbour a number of Dutch coasting vessels, also some German prizes, were anchored.

We were anchored in Plymouth for about six hours and all the transports were brought in. Then we were towed up the river to Devonport in a string. The *S.S. Laurentic* was near the head of the column and as we passed each bend, bringing the quays into view, we saw crowds of people. They certainly gave us a great reception. We could hear them cheering, but it was too far away to make anybody out or hear a band if they had one. All the way the boats and dockyards blew their whistles and the men-o'-war and training ships had their crews out to man the decks.

We finally anchored opposite Devonport. Our sister ship, *S.S. Megantic*, was attached alongside of us with cables. The *Megantic* had the 48th Highlanders of Toronto on board, and the 31st Regiment of North Grey, also wearing kilts. The 31st were attached to the 1st Battalion in Val Cartier and I was their sergeant, so I knew them all.

The *Laurentic* was not docked for five days. We had very short rations the last couple of days and tobacco and matches gave out altogether. The reason we were held up so long was that the railways were unable to handle such a large number of men, and so only a few thousand were let off at a time, marched to the station and shipped to the depot nearest their camp. If they had let the Canadians run loose through the city until they could transport them, half our gallant army would be lost yet!

At noon on the fifth day, our troop landed and marched out to the *Laconia* which had carried the horses. I wish you could have seen and smelt the *Laconia*! It was a floating sewer and the men who were unfortunate enough to have gone with the horses deserve a V.C. They only lost sixteen horses (at $175 each)—a very low number considering the time it took to make the crossing.

After obtaining our horses off the boat, we led two each (they were in no condition to ride) to the station a couple of miles away. (Crowds in the streets seemed to think we were going to the front at once.) We got our horses entrained by midnight and at six next morning reached Amesbury—twelve miles from Pond Farm Camp on Salisbury Plains which was to be our happy home.

SALISBURY PLAIN

Salisbury Plain, about fifteen miles square, is like Western Canada: rolling country covered with short grass, a few large clumps of trees and several beautiful country homes, now in ruins: broken windows, no roofs and huge gaps in the walls. (They say that when Pond Farm was taken over by the government, these houses were used as targets by the artillery.)

There are a number of sham batteries hereabouts with trenches and sheds behind them. The ground is all torn up and scored by shells. I saw empty shrapnel cases in different places, which had failed to explode. There are also wooden targets representing men in different attitudes (standing, kneeling and lying) at points all over the hillsides.

Large flocks of sheep and some cattle graze on the hills. A few small houses are left, most likely the homes of shepherds. This never was farming country as it is all chalk about four inches below the surface.

The camp is roughly divided into three parts used by the Canadian Contingent: "Pond Farm" (for the Cavalry, Royal Canadians and Strathconas, also a few battalions of infantry including the Newfoundlanders), "West Down South" (for Army Service Mechanical Transports, Ammunition Columns, Artillery and other mounted units) and "Bustard Camp," which is Headquarters and has nearly all the Medical Corps including a Field Hospital. Canadians are the only troops under canvas in England.

Our tents are not as good as those we had in Canada and often leak when it rains. They have wooden floors laid down in four sections. We looked on this as a great luxury at first, but we soon found it was a necessity. Of course it is not as soft to sleep on as the ground, but they looked so clean and so easy to keep clean, that everybody was delighted and when we were issued with canvas palliasses (which are ticks to be filled with straw and used as mattresses) we thought we had struck a model camp.

We soon found out our mistake. I have not seen any straw in camp yet and we were refused permission to fill our ticks with hay, as there is sometimes not enough for the horses. The wooden floors were necessary; without them the rain would soon have swamped us.

For the first month it rained every single day except the Sunday we arrived. We have been inspected several times and generally in a rainstorm. As some humorist has remarked, we go out for an inspection and find that it is a bathing parade instead.

We have been inspected a number of times by Gen. Alderson (who is in charge of the Canadian Contingent), once by Lord Roberts, since dead, and by the King accompanied by Lord Kitchener and staff, with several ladies. I do not know if the Queen was amongst the party or not.

On every occasion, we were kept waiting on horseback for at least an hour (and once for three hours) without cloaks in a miserable cold rainstorm. We also had the horror of being addressed one Sunday by an Archbishop, a most distinguished old mutt, who tired us all to death talking about the "Powah of prayah" and a lot of other useful dope. It is just astonishing how important some of these ministers think their messages are and on the only day of rest we get they keep us on parade listening to a sermon.

TRAINING AT POND FARM

It snowed last night. The change in weather is very agreeable as we are able to leave the horse lines down. We were obliged to change them every two or three days because the horses stood in pools of water where they had stamped the ground to pieces. We moved them so often that we finally got them a good fifteen minutes walk from our tents. Now we have moved them (I hope) for the last time in this camp.

We do most of our riding in the morning and we generally ride hard and fast. We have had all our troop drill and now work in squadrons and regimental drill once or twice a week. We will soon get manoeuvres extending over three to six days. Also there is a mounted patrol every night in some one or other of the towns here to round up any drunks or loafers who have left camp without leave.

I have been once to Devizes, seven miles from here. I saw recruits for Kitchener's army there, dressed in a black uniform which looked as though it had been pasted together. (They said that some of their number had been taken up as escaped convicts, before the police became accustomed to the uniform.)

The Commander in Chief issued orders that 20% of the soldiers be permitted passes on weekends and 5% be given six-day passes. London is the Happy Hunting Ground of the colonial soldier on pass. About a thousand never waited for passes at all and another thousand thought their weekend passes were good until their money ran out or they could no longer dodge the London Police.

The result is that weekend passes were reduced to 10%, but still London is overrun with Canadian soldiers (absent without leave) who are practically beggars. Some of them meet the trains begging for a few pence; even a copper is not despised and they have sold

The Teaban family in about 1900, John second from left

half their uniforms; it is not uncommon to see Canadians dressed in semi-military fashion with overalls, serge and bowler hat, or wearing a ragged smock instead of greatcoat. The prize was taken by a Highlander who was found at large without a kilt, wearing a sailor hat and one spur! The Highlanders seem to be the worst, but possibly their uniform makes them more conspicuous.

The excuses they give are very original. One of the RCDs took his horse off the line; on his return he told the Colonel that he is a somnambulist and all he remembered was waking up one morning on horseback in a strange part of the country. Another old soldier accompanied a friend on the train and was just saying goodbye when a Salvation Army band came along and started playing the National Anthem. Of course he was obliged to stand to attention and the train pulled out with him on board.

Among my duties here is "Provost," a daily duty to keep the prisoners at all the fatigues possible. At one time, fatigue work was lifting a heavy cannon ball without bending the knees, marching six paces and putting it down; marching another six paces, picking another up, and so on (one or two hours in the morning, and ditto in the afternoon, for a number of days). However a prisoner broke his back at this sort of sport once and, ever since, they have been given necessary fatigues around the camp.

Yesterday I had sixteen prisoners handed over to me. The interesting ones were the old soldiers who had four or five charges against them at one time. Their line of conversation was good. Real good. Some of them frankly stated that they intended to cut up capers until the RCDs got so sick of them that they would be given their papers—or, as one fellow put it, "an $8 suit and a ticket to Toronto!"

We received the straw for our palliasses last Wednesday and our beds are now comfortable—quite a difference to the bare floor.

We found the English money system hard at first, and I am not used entirely to it yet. The Government pays us a pound for $5.00 and four shillings for a dollar; this, of course, cheats us out of 4¢ on every dollar, but we were told that back in Canada the difference would be made up to us. In the Canteen, a nickel is only worth 4¢, to their way of figuring.

We have not been issued with either rifles or carbines yet, and even the officers are not sure which weapons we are finally to get, while we have only swords enough to arm the front rank of my section. It seems as though we will never be ready for the front.

DRAWING STORES

December 3, 1914. Was detailed as corporal in charge of Transport Waggons to go to West Down North today to draw one day's supplies for the regiment of 611 men and about 650 horses. There the mud was the worst I have seen yet: nowhere less than shoe-top deep, and in some places I sank nearly to my knees in slime.

There was a storm last night and several of the big marquees were down. My duty was to take the requisition of the RQM for coal and wood, meat and groceries, candles and vegetables. These come from different tents; at each one the Clerk puts on his share of the supplies called for, and you move on to another tent.

First was the bread marquee. Six men lined up and threw bunches of loaves at each other. No-one had clean hands and some were so awfully dirty that I never objected when any of the loaves fell in the mud. Sometimes a mud bath improved them and, anyway, the bread was piled on a horse blanket in the waggon.

The next stop was like a wholesale grocer's, only not so clean of course. Part of our daily ration was one pound of candles—I would like to find out some time who gets these!

At the fuel department, they had a Guard tent perched on a wood pile and a detachment of half-frozen Highlanders with very, very red knees were taking over the guard from an equally despondent-looking bunch from some other battalion. It was about the sorriest looking picture of the manly art of warfare that I ever saw!

At the butchers' waggons, the head butcher had arranged boxes in a sort of path from the waggon to the scales and his assistants nimbly leaped from box to box like sprightly goats, from crag to crag. The boxes were a good jump apart, and the fat butchers made a pretty sight merrily skipping along, each with a huge piece of beef on his shoulders.

After dinner I beat it out of camp without the formality of asking for leave. We spent a pleasant day in Market Lavington. ML has not an unmarried man left who can pass the standard required for the Army.

LIVING OUTDOORS

December 4, 1914. I do not see how they can expect the horses to live here. It is blowing a blizzard outside, and the poor animals are just standing and shaking. The ground is a mass of fast-freezing mud and it is almost more than we can do to keep their blankets on them. We found three horses from other squadrons wandering loose, and put them on our lines.

December 5, 1914. Moving the horse lines is a dirty job. There does not seem to be any ground around here where the horses have not been picketed and the only thing we can do is either move ourselves, or take them so far away that it will be an all-day job simply to march to the horse lines and back to our tents. The chalk under the grass will not soak up the water and it rains continually.

The whole camp is mud. Some places it is like putty but where there is much walking (like in front of tents) it is like thick soup. In fact, we have it in all degrees and depths from four to eighteen inches.

Nearly the whole regiment has purchased rubber boots. The only trouble is that they raise blisters on the heels and ankles. A few idiots wore them until they could not walk.

Most tents have purchased coal-oil heaters. Besides keeping the tent dry, we use ours for boiling coffee and making toast. Oil is worth a shilling a gallon and the stoves uses about two gallons in five days. We can get daily papers, chocolate, soap, butter and cake, tea, etc. at the dry canteen. A van comes every day, too, with stoves, boots, gloves, etc.

When the contingent first came over, Col. Sam Hughes intended that the camps should be "dry" the same as they were in Val Cartier, but Gen. Alderson interceded, and wet canteens were granted. At first ours was open for an hour at noon and from six to nine, but the Staff soon found that the men had time to get drunk during the noon hour and also got too vociferous at night. So the hours were cut to a half an hour at noon on Saturdays and Sundays, ten minutes other days and one hour every night.

December 6, 1914. Sunday—a holiday, which means that we forego the usual Riding Parade in the morning and the Grazing and Grooming Parade in the afternoon. However, I have not yet been able to look on any day as a holiday where you attend three stables, three times!

Up to last Sunday everyone was paraded to open-air church services but last Sunday the Roman Catholics kicked on going to the General Church Services, so the Sgt Major asked all the RCs to drop to the rear of the parade and dismissed us. He said that in future we would have to parade but when the squadron moved off we would be dismissed. This morning when he called for the RCs to fall out, the whole squadron tried to beat it. They were soon called back and, upon investigation, the tougher members of the squadron (including all the rough nuts who never were in church) were permitted to fall out.

I heard today we will all be sent on to the continent in January. Certainly if they do not send us to other quarters soon we might as well be in Germany. Salisbury is so miserable that it is not surprising that men overstay their passes or take French Leave for a week or two.

The wonder is that half the regiment has not deserted! London is full of deserters. I saw in the London papers that a sergeant from a Canadian Contingent was arrested for begging on the streets. The boys who have been in London say that they are afraid to meet soldiers with Maple Leaf badges in their caps, as half of them ask for handouts.

Quite a number of soldiers have got married. They go away on a three-day pass, meet their affinity the first day, marry her the second and return to duty the next day. Some of the Janes imagine that they will be entitled to the separation allowance for wives of Canadian soldiers on service, but such is not the case and it was read out in Regimental Orders that soldiers getting married need not expect a separation allowance or even a pension for their (English) wives in case they become widows.

However that does not discourage our gay bachelors at all. Only today one of the squadron toughs got a pass for two days. He is to be married tomorrow to a girl he saw for about half an hour when he deserted for a few days. She came to see him on his return and had a touching interview with him in the Guard House where he was doing cells. I saw her myself, as I was Provost that day, and she was very good-looking.

December 7, 1914. You should see our tents. They are pigpens. Seven men sleep in my tent, of which I am in charge. The tent is a regular bell, about twelve feet in diameter. Straw leaking out of half the mattresses mixes with the mud brought in every day. Around the tent pole is a dirty conglomeration of jam tins, rubber boots, muddy puttees, dirty socks, towels and spurs. A rope is fastened to the tent pole over which there are always a half-dozen wet overcoats hanging. The pole is decorated with haversacks and rusty swords. (It is impossible to keep the swords polished and we rub them over with emery paper every day. If we file them much more there will not be any blade left.)

When I came they used a slop barrel for waste paper, what mud they scraped off the floor, etc., and this they emptied when full. Now the barrel is outside the tent and the space is taken up with a litter of water bottles, mess tins and other junk. Our tent is by no means the worst; some of them have a most horrible odour. We will not be sorry to leave this place for France.

Reveille blows at 6:30 every morning and we go to stables at 6:45. Cookhouse blows at 8 a.m. and we get bread and bacon and tea without milk or sugar. Butter is never served.

We go on parade about 8:30 and ride till 12:30. Then, noon stables and dinner. Dinner is always stew. This noon I could not eat it and, not having time to empty my mess tin, I let it go until supper time when it was just a lot of grease. Looked like home made soap!

About 2 p.m. we groom the horses and then lead them out to graze until evening stables. Supper at five o'clock is bread, cheese and tea. (We buy butter from the canteen for our tent and pretty nearly live on toast and cheese.)

December 8, 1914. We had a very violent hail storm at noon followed by rain.

December 9, 1914. Very foggy. About two weeks ago, a squadron of Elliott's Horse from British Columbia, numbering about 80 men, came out and these are being taken into the Cavalry; we are now over strength and the undesirables are being culled out, sent to the Infantry or given a discharge on account of being unfit for cavalry work.

They say that Canadian Cavalry are to be used as a base for the Imperial Cavalry regiments. This means that when a British regiment is badly depleted, our men will be sent to take their places. There is, therefore, little chance of our being used for some time to come as all the fighting is being done in the trenches now, and there will be no serious advances until Spring when the Cavalry will be needed.

December 10, 1914. I heard tonight that all the mounted corps would be called out just before midnight to either make or repel an attack. (Just practise, of course.) I am glad I got a pass into town, as I have no desire to saddle my Polly in the dark.

DIVERSIONS

I came into the village to go to a dance. I wanted to see what kind of figure was cut by an unwashed cavalryman dancing in rubber boots with spurs on. They tell me they can dance first rate—two-step, waltz and square dances! The Hesitation, Turkey Trot and Tango have not reached these villages as yet.

McColl of 2nd troop C was in town, too. He was coatless, hatless and unmindful of the rain. He admitted being in London on a furlough which he granted to himself. McColl is quite a card. He is generally doing cells in the guard house. (A funny thing about these deserters is that they always want to get their ticket of discharge and wonder why they joined the Army, but they always come back after a week or so.)

December 12, 1914. Was Provost today. Took over four prisoners to load hay and oat waggons. At two o'clock, McColl joined our ranks. He got fourteen days Field Punishment. I always feel sorry for McColl—he is so miserable-looking. He is a South African veteran, and a fine example of a booze artist. He had no overcoat nor shoelaces in his poor-looking shoes today and this was no day to be half-dressed. The fog was so thick you could not see over 100 yards in any direction and the cold mist left an icy coating all over our clothes.

This Provost's job is quite a lazy one. All you have to do is take the prisoners over from the guard in the morning and set them to work while you stand and watch them. My prisoners have never given me any trouble (so far) and I can always get a man to help me if I ask.

December 13, 1914. This morning was so foggy that we could hardly find our way to the horse lines, but it cleared up later—

which was lucky as we moved the lines again this morning. They are now a long way from the tents and we have three steep muddy hills to cross to reach them.

There has been a lot of sickness lately, brought on by the wet weather and inability of the men to keep their feet and clothes dry. Today there were six cases in our troop of 38 men.

December 14, 1914. This has been a fine day and we took advantage of it to move our tents nearer the horse lines; also it is on the road to Lavington and will save steps when we want to go in; the best of it is that we are out of the mud for some time to come anyhow!

December 15, 1914. This afternoon was a half-holiday—and then most of the men were detailed on fatigues to fix up the new cookhouse and put up marquees for us to eat in. Carpenters are working on a couple of buildings which will be our canteens. In Canada, they would not last ten minutes! The huts came in pieces, windows and doors built into the walls, yet the carpenters work as though they were making the lumber first.

December 16, 1914. Had a sham battle today. We were with the attacking team. When we came up with the enemy the order was given to charge and both teams charged each other at full speed and in close order. It was a very realistic affair and it is a wonder we have not got a lot of dead soldiers and horses tonight. Luckily we managed to drive through each other's lines without serious damage. If anybody had ever told me we could pull off such a sham charge without causing real good men being suddenly transformed into cadavers, I would have said he was crazy! We have made exciting charges before—when there was nobody in front of us.

Would go into Lavington tonight, only all our troop who have swords are obliged to parade with the picket tonight for having that trusty weapon in a "Rusty, Dirty and otherwise Poor condition, greatly to the detriment of Military Discipline, etc...."

8 p.m. Lavington Market. The Strathconas have received orders to hold themselves in readiness to go to Boulogne. All leaves of absence are ended by January 8th. Boulogne is the military base of the Allies in Eastern Europe and most likely all the Canadian cavalry will train there for some time and then be used as guards to transports, etc. It's an even chance that we never get into action at all.

As I was leaving Lavington tonight about 8:45, an old man came along with a ladder which he solemnly placed underneath a street lamp and then, climbing the ladder, blew the light out. He told me that he always started to put the lights out at 8:30 and finished his rounds at 9 o'clock. He said "Nobody with any self respect would be out on the streets after that hour!" (You might tip George and Frank *{brothers}* off to that!).

December 10, 1914. We had one of the roughest rides to do I ever went through. It was a bareback exercise ride of about seven miles and the horses did not even have a blanket or surcingle on them. We walked, trotted, jogged, galloped and went through every possible gait guaranteed to torture a man.

We were obliged to lead one horse on the headrope only and this is sometimes pretty hard to do even when you have a saddle. We also climbed several hills about ten feet high which were almost perpendicular.

ON LEAVE IN LONDON

December 20, 1914. YMCA Tottenham Court Road London London is full of soldiers and sailors. About 70% of the soldiers are Canadians and they seem to be very popular. The city has many Belgian refugees, also a few wounded soldiers on leave.

Nobody takes the war to heart much and the general impression seems to be that the Germans have their backbone badly bent and that about midsummer at the latest the Allies will break them altogether.

A few days ago, I met Mr. Robbins of Walkerville. He told me that the Windsor Chapter of the Daughters of the Empire were going to give each Windsor soldier a box of cigarettes or wooden nutmegs or some other blawsted thing. I have not received a nickel's worth of stuff from the people of Windsor with the exception of corn-cob pipes and Old Chum Smoking tobacco (which I gave to the First Hussars) since I left home and I do not want any! I have money enough to buy my own shirts, etc. When I go back, I do not wish any of the Daughters of the Empire to look at my feet and say "How did you like those socks I sent you?"

December 21, 1914. Quite a number of soldiers were drilling in and around the Tower; in fact, nearly every vacant lot and park has a bunch at work with maxims, signalling apparatus, etc. Nearly all are in uniform but one or two new recruits are in civilian clothes.

I am in one of J. Lyons & Co.'s famous tea shops which are scattered all over London thicker than Boston Lunches in Detroit....

I got an ice cream soda up the Strand last night. *Hurray!* It was served by a dignified man in a drug store who went over the list as though he was reading a death sentence. I believe he had four flavours. He told me that American Cold Drinks, as they call them, did not take very well in England. After I took my dose, I believed him!

December 22, 1914. In a barber shop. London is posted with signs calling volunteers for the Second Million Army. Every store and many private homes have them in the windows, while every taxicab and bus has a poster on the front.

23 December, 1914. On the Great Western Railway Express. At supper at the Union Jack Club last night, I met a sergeant from the RCHA and a friend of his, Trudell by name. Trudell could not speak English and, after asking my permission, they jabbered along in real old Canadian French. It was as good as a show to me. It reminded me of the euchre parties in the Immaculate Conception [Church] when your opponents told each other their hands.

BACK IN CAMP

December 24, 1914. Pond Farm Camp. I found our camp fairly deserted. At least a third of our squadron were granted passes for Xmas, the balance for New Years. They have been doing no drilling for the last few days, but merely take exercise rides, one man leading three horses. In the afternoons there were the regular fatigue parties and the balance were set to work decorating a large hut on the hill where we shall have Xmas dinner.

One of our trumpeters is on leave and the other so far forgot himself as to call the Sgt Major a — liar, and so is in the booby hatch again. So Vic Spaulding of the Third Troop who has not played a note on a trumpet for years is our bugler. When I first heard the calls, I had to laugh, I was so sure the bugler was drunk.

Xmas Eve. In Guard House over Pumping Station. A beautiful moonlit night with stars and the ground is barely covered with snow. The sides of the tent are frozen stiff; the gasoline engine in the bomb-proof pumphouse coughs away and I can hear the footsteps of my sentry Jim Ormiston cracking away as he walks his beat.

I have charge of three in all. The other two, Wilson and Pierce are trying to light a bonfire to warm some tea. The only wood they have is green branches and they have been working for some time to coax up a miserable flame. They wanted to go to an old barn and rip down some boards but, as I had been warned of a well, very lightly covered in front of the house, I forbade them going.

Jim Ormiston, an old soldier, tells me with great emotion, that this is the first time he has ever had to stand guard Xmas Eve. So I told the others that we should feel flattered to be able to do in our first year what an old soldier never did in ten years service. Absolutely hopeless! They did not see the humour in it at all.

There was collected off of each of C Squadron today 1/6 to pay for Xmas dinner tomorrow. A waggon went all the way to Devizes for a piano to be used after dinner. Some of the boys get fearfully homesick when they come back to camp after a pass.

Pierce has just come in and his overcoat is frozen stiff. We are quite comfortable in this tent which is well bedded down with hay; also we have a lantern, which is quite a luxury.

The general opinion of wounded men returned from the front is that the war will be over by April. The English I have met certainly take the war very calmly. No-one doubts for one minute that the Allies will be successful and although London is darkened at night and Buckingham Palace, Admiralty, Whitehall, etc. have searchlights and maxims on the roof, everyone would be exceedingly surprised if a Zeppelin was ever discovered.

Xmas morning, 1914. 9 o'clock—Just going to get up. This Pump House Guard is a snap and we could not have an easier Xmas Day in camp. Wilson, who should have better sense, complains that he entirely forgot to hang up his stocking last night. However, if his socks are like the majority I have seen they are not fit to hang up.

The Orderly Officer paid us a visit last night and after he was gone, I permitted the guard to turn in for the night, only turning a sentry out once for First Post a quarter of an hour after lights out. I did this as so many drunks were returning from camp from LM; even this morning, little bands of visitors continued coming in. Several came to the guard tent to enquire the way to their squadron lines. Many were singing the popular songs of the day—"Tipperary," "Lonesome Pine," "Girl in Heart of Maryland" and one lone wayfarer made a howling success of "Please don't take me Home." We all slept till until a few minutes ago when Jim Ormiston, who is our cook, bestirred himself and is now getting fire ready for breakfast....

We had our breakfasts outside this morning in front of the bonfire which we rigged up with an old tin kettle and a piece of tin with edges turned up to fry our bacon in. The morning was very fine and we had a real jolly breakfast—more like a picnic than anything I have had in this country yet, and will be something to look back to.

5:15 p.m. We were disappointed in coming off guard to find that Xmas dinner had been pulled off at noon today, but we made the best we could of a cold supper and I must say the boys took it in good part.

I was mistaken about there being no drunks in our lines. I am now in the new canteen and there are fourteen or fifteen gentlemen of the RCDs who are really hilarious and as many more in their tents quite dead to the world, so I am creditably informed. They have a well tuned piano in here, and I have been playing accompaniments to the songs and dances of the small crowd here already....

Trooper Twine of Windsor is just now reciting the soldier's favourite "The Face on the Bar Room Floor." The favourite part as far as the RCDs seem concerned is the bar room floor!

9 p.m. Returned to my tent. The happy gathering in the mess house were practically stupefied when I left and four or five were on their backs in the middle of "The bar room floor."

December 26, 1914. Bitterly cold and pouring rain since early this morning. Morning stables was almost a farce, there were so few men on the job and the Sergeants did not turn up at all. The poor horses stood shivering with their backs to the rain and wind, and many had their blankets half off as usual. It is pitiful to see them huddle together.

Parish Room M.L. 9 p.m. Took a little pass for myself tonight to have tea in town. It was a great success. I find that with practice I am able to make the trip into the village in about 40 minutes, and so arrived in here sharp at 6 o'clock. Had a fine supper of steak and onions with a dessert of cornstarch pudding garnished with an immense dish of dried peach preserves and two cups of cocoa.

Later I went to the barber's, but this gentleman was so drunk and shaky that I left before my turn and went to the Lady Barber's. The lady in charge, who weighs about 200 pounds at ringside, gave me the fastest shave I have ever had.

NEWS FROM THE FRONT

I ran into a man from the 6th Royal Horse Artillery (Imperial Service). He had just returned wounded. He told us that his Battalion left Salisbury on Wednesday morning and on Friday noon were shelling the Germans. They took part in the retirement of Mons and subsequent engagements with a total loss of six men killed or wounded. At Mons, the Germans advanced in such close order and such masses that the 6th used Fuse-Nought ammunition at a range of less than 300 yards. Fuse-0 means ammunition that, immediately after leaving the mouth of the guns, which were eighteen lbs, spreads with a radius of 50 yards.

The mortality among the Germans was something awful, he says, and only their numbers and rapid advance saved them from little short of a massacre. As it was, their losses were terrible, as the British Cavalry charged repeatedly, following the artillery fire. However the allies were obliged to retreat for a full sixteen days on account of being outnumbered ten to one. This is one of the longest retreats in history in which the retreating force fairly outslaughtered the pursuers. Now it is the Germans who are retreating.

This battery made a new record in point of shells fired from a four-gun battery in the course of one day: number of shots being 1500. He says it takes eighteen horses to haul one waggon load of ammunition up to the fire trenches, which are well covered and concealed. The state of the roads are fierce and rain storms are continuous, no doubt caused by unceasing heavy firing.

His only real complaint was lack of washing accommodations. In sixteen days, he only had one wash and that in a muddy Jack Johnson hole. A Jack Johnson hole is a gap in the earth caused by a shell, and when this fills with water, the soldiers use it as a bathtub.

We moved our cookhouse today up to the new hut where we are going to eat all our meals after this at tables. I had charge of the morning fatigue party and when I went to see how the scrubbers and swabbers were getting on, they insisted that I play the piano and they would not work unless I played some fast tunes. By the time the job was done, I was as tired as they claim to have been refreshed.

Very cold tonight but a clear starlit night. Had a great walk back, arriving after 11 o'clock. Met a drunken trooper from the ammunition column at the foot of the long hill and between pulling and shoving I finally managed to get him to the top and was then forced to carry the old coot about a mile to get him started on his way back to camp. After leaving him, I cut across the downs and you could hardly see more than ten yards. My clothes were soon soaked through with mist.

Came across another souse from the RCDs who was coming back from a little celebration at the Strathconas lines. He swore he had been lost for hours. I had great pleasure in pointing out the wet canteen to him and he got his true bearings at last. The wet canteen is a landmark most of our men are thoroughly acquainted with. (I cannot understand why a number of men have not either frozen to death or broken their necks coming over the downs when the mist comes up so fast. It is clear one minute and the next you are enveloped in thick, watery, white clouds.)

RAIN AND SNOW

December 27, 1914. Rained and sleeted nearly all morning. When we went to stables at 6:30 only a few men seemed to be present. I had to take over the 4th troop as I suppose Sgt Olmstead had not recovered from last night's souse. The horse lines were changed on Xmas eve, yet they are worse than a swamp. We moved them about 11 o'clock and the Protestants were therefore excused from going to church.

8 p.m. Raining heavily for last hour. Was over to the dry canteen tonight and there were only three other customers. We are no great distance from the marquee, but there is an immense sheet of heavy, deep mud between us and no-one will go over there unless they have to.

Many soldiers have cut their long military riding coats or cloaks down from the knees, as the bottoms were caked with mud which made mounting and walking difficult; so now the regiment appears to be wearing Prince Albert coats and if they had silk hats would look like the Chicago section of the Elks parade!

December 28, 1914. The horse blankets issued at Val Cartier are now in fierce shape: buckles and straps are gone and some are a handful of rags. Headstalls, ropes and halters also have frayed out and sometimes we have to use hay wire or two or three nosebags hung together.

7:45 p.m. Snowing hard tonight, so strong as to penetrate the tent like rain. We have tightened up all the guy ropes to prevent our happy home from falling down with weight of snow.... Surely they cannot keep us on the Plains much longer if this continues.

...Nine men from C squad were had up for being in Devizes without a pass. They were brought to Bustard Camp Guard House overnight, where they amused themselves trying to keep warm. To do this they were obliged to break up the tables and benches and so kept a good fire going all night. They got off with loss of one day's pay and other comparatively light sentences.

The prisoners are grateful that it was not the Strathconas who brought them back. The Straths have a pleasant habit of tying a prisoner's hands together around one stirrup. It is not so bad when walking but when the horse begins to trot or canter, some of the experienced ones tell me, it is an entirely different matter

While on the morning's ride we passed a number of very elaborate trenches and barb wire entanglements which were newly constructed by the engineers. They certainly had some job trenching in the chalk but they made fine jobs of the work.

There has been an awful sale of Keating's Insect Powder at the canteen lately. Everyone is using it in large quantities.

December 29, 1914. Bitterly cold all morning. Lieut. Broome came back from his holidays this morning and we are very sorry to see him. He is one man who I feel absolutely sure will not come back to Canada at the close of the war. In fact, he will not go anyplace to judge by his popularity in this squadron. Even Maj. MacMillan takes pleasure in insulting him before the squadron, and if he really happens to live through the campaign I myself will certainly beat him to a frazzle when we get once more into civilians. My muscles fairly ache when I think of slashing him a wallop on the nose.

The wet canteen blew down last night and some of the empty beer kegs caught fire. The two men in the tent narrowly escaped being burned up. This the fourth time this has happened to the wet canteen.

They have been using Second Field Punishment in some of the battalions but it has been stopped by Gen. Alderson. The punishment consisted of being tied when off duty to a cart wheel, two hours on and two off, up to about 8:30 at night. The weather has never been very good here for that kind of exercise.

December 30, 1914. Was Provost today and have eight bad men on my hands. Worked them successfully this morning but they are a mutinous crew and some are just working for their tickets.

My old friend McColl, who spent about three quarters of his time in the Guard House, is back again and has received his discharge. He is only awaiting his $8.00 suit of clothes when he will be escorted to the extreme end of the camp and kicked out.

At noon I received letters from Patsy {sister}, Mother, postcards from Angela, Brydie Breen and Mrs. Tiernan; also your oatmeal biscuits & peanut butter. I am glad to hear that Mother intends coming to England this summer after peace is declared. I am getting to know quite a lot about it and can even think and speak in l.s.d., while London is easier to me than the blocks behind the Detroit Public Library.

NEW YEAR'S DAY 1915

New Year's Day, 1915. At midnight, there was a few faint cheers and some notes played on the trumpet. No other noise was heard in this camp, likely on account of the wet canteen closing at the usual hour.

Freezing and blowing a hurricane this morning. It is impossible to keep the horse blankets on in some of these storms and you can hear them crying out most piteously. If these rains keep up the German fleet will sail up on Salisbury plains and bombard the Canadian Contingent!

6 p.m. Main Guard Tents. It has rained steadily from four o'clock this morning and the ground is most miserable to walk on, while the tents and floors are soaked through and slippery and slimy mud.

Kelly and Blain, both friends of mine, are my "guests" tonight. Both have drawn fifteen days Field Punishment. Trooper Wren, a former reporter on the Montreal Star (also a "late" lieutenant in the Engineers which disbanded in Val Cartier) spent a pleasant morning with me. He is doing Field Punishment #2 but drew in addition five days CB for sleeping today. Confinement to Barracks gives the defaulter extra fatigues. Also, starting at 6 p.m., the Defaulter call is blown every half hour up to 9 which the defaulters have to answer. The prisoner has just time to go into his tent when he is called out again—and in all sorts of weather. After five days C.B. a man can run 200 yards in about fifteen seconds flat.

My old friend McColl is still in the clink and I heard in the orderly room that he and three others will get their $8.00 suits on Monday. I heard Capt. Gilman tell the orderly Sergeant that if he could buy suits for less, to get them! Size is no object; a six footer generally gets a suit meant for a five footer, and vice versa.

McColl put a sign up on the prisoners' tent "Abandon soap, All ye who enter here." It might well be copied by the entire regiment.

MOVING INDOORS

January 3, 1915. 1 p.m. This tent might just as well have no top to it. The rain is running from the door to the tent pole in a stream and at the centre it leaks under the wooden floor which is tilted at any old angle. The entrance is a foot higher than the center, which adds to the charm of this particular pig sty. You never know when entering just what part of the anatomy you will light on when your legs slip from under you on the greasy, slimy floor; also it is great fun to watch strangers enter or exit.

Tomorrow we leave our humble abode for a village. A fatigue party has gone ahead to clean the stables and get things in readiness.

"No Church Parade" sounded on the trumpet brought hearty cheers from all. The Sgt Major made a little speech after stables last night in which he said that no more passes would be granted, and that all would have to get right down to work and "play the game" and "be soldiers," etc., etc. Said also that we had had our little holiday. The S.M.'s idea of a holiday is really humorous and as for being

John Patrick Teahan in 1914

Soldiers, we will be glad to have a change from Sailor life on Salisbury Plains.

A half-witted specimen in the Second Troop called "Slim" Porter has gone crazy at last. He is just now outside, bareheaded and unmindful of the pouring rain, busy tossing a ring of hay wire in the air and catching it on the end of a stick.

January 4, 1915. Shrewton, Wiltshire. Ground was covered with a snowy slush this morning and air was raw and chilly. After breakfast we held a sort of improvised farewell concert in the mess where we still had the piano we rented for Xmas.

I had a terrible job on my hands to get the troop ready to leave the lines. I had to follow each man about and curse each and every one individually, finally having to put Roberts and Wade under Open Arrest. These are the first two I have tried to scalp so far. I turned them over to Mr. Broome who swore artistically and enthusiastically, using entirely novel expressions in regard to everybody, not excepting myself.

I was amazed at the condition of the country which was simply flooded. Every valley was a chain of lakes and rivers and several times the water came so high on the horses' sides that if I had not been wearing rubber boots, my feet would have got wet. The roads in dozens of places were rivers with rapid currents.

We arrived about 4:30 and have a fine, roomy barn in a picturesque old place once used as a racing stable and called Pratt's Stables. Across the yard is a tack room with plenty of room for all saddlery and it contains a small coal oil stove. The horses have been put three in a loose box and are left untied and without blankets. They will soon pick up here and some actually grinned when we led them into their boxes. It sure was time for a change: a few weeks more of Pond Farm and we would have had to haul half of them to the dump. In the last storm, I saw two horses fall over when their blankets were pulled straight, and some just had life enough in them to reach here.

If the horses have fared well, the men have reached Paradise. We are billeted in houses and have our meals served to us just like home. I am in charge of ten men in a vacant cottage, part of a row of terraces, and as nice a clean and neat little apartment you never saw. Thatched roof, whitewashed walls, narrow tiled walk and small garden in front. Just like a picture.

The downstairs consists of one room with a big fireplace. The floor is of big, clean-looking bricks. With two benches and coats on nails in the wall, the room looks real home-like. The finishing touch is an alarm clock which I purchased tonight for a half crown and is now ticking away over the fireplace. A short flight of steps leads to our sleeping quarters.

With the exception of McKinley and Vic Cumminsky the gang I am commanding are considered the wasters of the troop and everybody laughed when they were read out in my charge. Three are in open arrest already, and I will be lucky if I am not obliged to hang a couple before we leave here.

Wade and Roberts were in the Guard tent this morning, doing cells on a fifteen-day sentence and were returned to duty on account of the move, and both of these heroes told me tonight that they would be glad to get their tickets. When a man is glad to get his ticket, the best and easiest method of dealing with him is to take him out and smite him one good wallop with a tent mallet. The balance of our gang are Pierce, Fischer, Newly, Wilson and Cooke. Some have done cells and those who have not were simply lucky.

We get our meals in two cottages in the same terrace: five in each one. I have picked the cleanest and most likely, Pierce and Wilson, to eat with McKinley, Cumminsky and myself. We have our meals at a Mrs Pierce's and she certainly feeds us high if tonight's supper is a fair example, which she said it was not as she did not expect us until tomorrow, She wanted to know if we were accustomed to four meals a day or only three. I was too dazed for to answer but at last managed to make her understand that the supper she served us tonight was more than equal to all the meals we ever had in camp and we would be very content with three such meals per day.

ROUTINES AND REGULATIONS

January 5, 1915. Have not got into routine yet, but made a start this morning by arising at 6:15 and arriving at stables by 6:45. Came back to a substantial breakfast at 8 a.m. and returned to stables at 9. Had a hard time to satisfy Mr Broome but think we had him pacified at the finish. He is, for the time being, Lord of all he surveys and is most exacting.

The stable management seems to be left entirely with me and I at once made myself popular with my choice coterie by driving them like the head of cattle they are. Wade, Roberts and Cooke have to be bullied and slugged like pigs, while Fischer, who is apparently simple-minded, goes about doing absolutely nothing, and wearing a simple smile on his dirty, unwashed face.

7:10 p.m. Have just received instructions from Sgt Walshe to have prisoners, evidence and guard mounted tomorrow and ready to ride to Amesbury. We are to be there by 2, when a number of cases will be dealt with.

We were told today that we will be here for two or three weeks, just sufficient time to get the horses and men recuperated for service and then we will be sent to France.

9:10 Our little cottage is crowded right now, and we have one visitor: Guitarrez, the Indian, arrived much under the influence and has let out a couple of war whoops. He has some cakes with him and is tearing huge hunks out of them, like a wolf. He has just been insulting Mr Broome, so he says.

January 7, 1915. After dinner we paraded prisoners, guard and evidence to Squadron Headquarters in Winterburn-Stokes, a village two or three miles from here. My prisoners were dealt with at once and found guilty of Insolence to a Superior Officer. Cooke got ten days First Field Punishment. Wade, asked for a court martial and was remanded for 24 hours to decide whether he would take the Major's sentence or not. Roberts took the Major's word and was admonished.

When I came out after giving evidence, Cooke made the mistake of saying he would get me yet, and get me good—so I had him re-arrested. On the Second Offence he got an additional 28 days, making 38 days with loss of pay to be spent in the nearest prison. This will be Aldershot and it is a real tough outlook.

Now that we are billeted, more attention has to be paid to the niceties of soldiering. Every man will now shave every day and keep his shoes, buttons, etc. polished; also, saddlery and swords must be spotless. Quite a change for some who on Salisbury Plains had not even washed for as long as a week.

January 8, 1915. McKinley got a letter returned to him by the Censor with a few remarks, checked by a blue pencil. He had mailed it to his wife in Toronto in which he gave the Canadian

Government a calling down for the way affairs in general were being handled, particularly in regards to his wife's Separation Allowance (she has not received a cent since he joined). Also the fact that we have not yet been issued with carbines or rifles and in many other things are more behind than some of the militia regiments who have been in camp only fourteen days.

January 8, 1915. On picket at the stables. Cumminsky was transferred from our billet tonight, to a more peaceful one. His place was taken by Cpl Shoeing Smith McLeod, who was kicked out of his other billet for being drunk all the time. I think we will have to rename our cottage "The Bum's Retreat."

Six hundred of Kitchener's Army left Salisbury yesterday for the front. All seem to be sent in similar detachments from time to time and take the place in the ranks of the casualties.

January 10, 1915. Fine bright brisk morning and birds are out making a prodigious noise. Jackdaws, larks, starlings, thrushes, etc., all new to the Canadians, make the village seem like an aviary.

9 p.m. Have been trying to read for the best part of an hour but the saloons closing at 8 p.m. the two corporals had nowhere to go but home and they have been having a foolish drunken argument for the past hour. This has become a regular habit and is making me wish to either have them transferred or taken out of active service—or shot. In fact when I look over these mutts I cannot decide that we would be any the loser if they were all shot. I for one will shed no tears over any of them.

January 11, 1914. Squadron Parade this morning on a hill about two miles from our stables. We rode out as far as Stonehenge passing a number of infantry columns on the road. On the left of the Amesbury Road about 500 yards from Stonehenge was a regular city of huts. I was surprised as the last time we came by there was only bare commons. The infantry companies who passed us looked fine and well set up—an entirely different aggregation to the bunch who first assembled in Canada.

40 men from the 7th Battalion died in one week from a disease which has the doctors puzzled. It is given out as spinal meningitis and is supposed to be caused by the dampness in the ground coming up impregnated with sulphur or similar substance and infecting the men.

January 12, 1915. Regimental parade today was cancelled and we had troop drill instead. Sgt Walshe put us through in great shape but all Broome could do was to give us riding school exercises. On Saturday next, we will have been on Salisbury Plains for four months and have in all five months service, yet none of us have received instruction with rifle or carbine, nor do we even know what we are to get. The only ones to carry swords are a few in the front rank and we have had no instruction in its use. In fact, we have wasted a lot of time in England so far.

January 13, 1915. Slight rain this morning. The artillery has been firing intermittently on the Plains these last two days, and this is being blamed for the large amount of rain which has been falling in England and causing floods. It is either the artillery here or effects of [artillery] fire in Belgium which might possibly be felt this far away.

We paraded to the Quarter Master's Stores this morning, and drew some socks (three pairs), a grey shirt and a handkerchief. I also received shoes, underclothes and Khaki breeches. (I will have a small departmental store stock before long simply because I cannot resist something for nothing.) We were told to get as much as we could as it would be our last chance. Jim Ormiston just tells me that he will use handkerchiefs for polishing rags as he has never used a handkerchief, so does not need one.

The Strathcona Horse have all been armed with the Long Ross Rifle, but they are not quite sure but that they might be handed bayonets and used in the trenches as infantry; however they are all armed with swords as well.

Col. Nelles is to be retired shortly, and no doubt things will move faster then. Gen. Alderson has ordered the retirement of over 70 Canadian officers for one reason or another.

January 14, 1915. Sutton of 3d Troop has been sending two pounds per month to a girl in Urchfont to whom he had become engaged. When he went to see her last Sunday, she had beat it with all his wealth—seven pounds (less than $35). Sutton is as heartbroken as such a muttonhead can be.

The infantry have been notified that they pull out on the 7th of Feb. and some artillery and mechanical transport have gone, while the poor old cavalry are left slobbering around with no aim—and incomplete equipment.

January 15, 1915. Two trees in front of the pub have been trimmed like cylinders standing on end with a bird perched on top of each. I do not know what kind of shrubbery it is but I would like to take some home to put around the house inside the stone fence in front.

"A" and "B" Squadrons are to be supplied with long Ross rifles next Thursday and will go to the ranges on the 21st and 22d of this month. There are not enough rifles to go around, so my "C" gets none.

Have applied for a transfer to "B" Sqdn. They cannot refuse to give a corporal permission to transfer if he is willing to revert, so I am sure that my application will go through.

January 17, 1915. The Elliott's Horse, which has been buffeted about between the RCDs and Light Strathcona Horse is finally being split between the squadrons of each regiment. There has been a lot of trouble with Elliott's Horse, through no fault of the E.H. troopers, and they are glad to get settled at last. Certainly the Cavalry could use them as there are vacancies in each squadron, but of course "C" Squadron will have their vacancies filled last. At present we have only about 25 men, instead of the 35 we left Canada with.

January 18, 1915. We are to be in billets in France too, but the infantry are to go into huts. The system is to send them into the trenches for about a week and then retire them to huts for another week to recuperate, so they will always be fresh. The Princess Patricias Light Infantry have been over there since Xmas and have had several casualties.

Lord Kitchener in an interview a few days ago said that he did not know when the war would end, but he expected it would be about the First of May if there were any Germans left.

8:30 p.m. On picket at stables. Cooke was telling me how he served six months in Simcoe jail, having been let off eighteen months on account of youth and good behaviour. Roberts then said he served four years in an English Reform school. Wade could not follow suit with such interesting history, but boasted about his father who had done several terms. They are a fine crew, alright.

January 19, 1915. A great number of companies, battalions and regiments have been doing a lot of route marching around here lately and it looks like a few preliminary "deceiving marches" preparatory to leaving for France; for instance, half of the 4th Battalion were marched away from camp loaded down with complete kit on several occasions; but when they had another route march the next thing we knew, they were in France!

My application for transfer to "B" was refused by Maj. MacMillan and he will grant no transfers whatever or even give discharges to some of those who wished them. I am now in wrong and am not only to lose my stripes but be sent to one of the other troops. ISCHCABIBBLE!

I am glad to get away from Lieut. Broome but sorry to leave the boys of the 4th. There is one satisfaction in hitting the bottom and that is that you have no place to go to but up again, and I have been promised my stripes back shortly, by the Sergeant Major.

Major MacMillan was quite peeved by the applications for transfer which started with me. However he said we would go to the front as soon as any of the other troops and there was no truth in the rumour that the RCDs and LSH were to be united.

"C" Squadron has had four or five deaths due from cold and exposure, and one man returned to Canada medically unfit as a result of that bareback ride we took before Xmas. He did not feel the effects at first but it turned out to be a very serious rupture. Altogether the Canadian Contingent has lost by deaths about 350 men since leaving Quebec. This is a very high rate and the Infantry has suffered the highest in numbers and percentages.

The boys in this troop have been going pretty hard on the booze since leaving Pond Farm. In fact, it was a mistake to open the canteens to the soldiers in the first place, as you would admit if you saw some of them before the canteens were opened, and the same fellows now—Adamski & Guitarrez have been drunk for weeks and Smith McLeod has not been sober for several months. As long as they do their work no-one complains.

January 20, 1915. Phillips of the QM Stores died this morning with double pneumonia. The average of late has increased to eight deaths per day among the entire contingent.

A queer thing about the soldiers is that each one solemnly announces that if he is alive at the end of the war he intends to get married at once and settle down, and many have married here in England already. I think that they are homesick and lonely and so will pick up with the first likely looking girl they meet. A private named Baker from a Western regiment married a Belgian girl in London after only a few days acquaintance in which an interpreter was needed to carry on a conversation. A paper, commenting on it, says that if neither one ever learns the other's language it should make an ideal marriage.

ARMS FOR THE TROOPS

January 21, 1915. "C" Squadron was paraded near Winterburn-Stokes this morning and Ross Rifles Mark II were given to about three quarters of each troop. The rifles are of 1910 pattern, not the improved model supplied to the infantry—although the "improved" model is not up to much and, as a mistake was made in the manufacture of their magazines, they can be used only as single shot rifles: the magazine will not hold the shell clip. However these may be only a temporary issue as the sights are for match (target) shooting and not active service sights.

We have no buckets, these having been turned in, nor any slings so we carry the rifle across the saddle or rest the butt on the toe of our right boots, holding the gun upright with our hands.

This was a Field Day and our squadron was supposed to retire before the attack of a battalion of infantry to a large hill and make a final stand there against a storming party. I suspect Mr Broome misunderstood orders as usual for later he was roundly cursed by the troop who said it would be suicide to follow him in active service.

January 22, 1915. Received a letter from Mother with newspaper clippings with my remarks in it and am still wondering why you were so foolish as to put my name in the paper at all. If the censors saw that you were being told that we had not a complete issue at this late date and that in other things we were away behind, they would soon stop all letters to Mrs D. Teahan until a few obliterations had been made. Anyhow, I do not need any free advertising. If Frank *(newspaperman brother)* wants to use any of this dope, do not use any names until the war is over.

January 24, 1915. Nearly all the 4th Troop got drunk last night at the Royal Oak Inn and made quite a disturbance. The picket were under the influence, while the Corporal was so far gone that he was put under open arrest & another man substituted in his place. There is going to be trouble if these drunken orgies continue.

8:30 p.m. Had a very cursory medical inspection at W-S this afternoon. The Doctor simply looked at us and said "You'll do."

The Fourth Troop were obliged to march over and back a distance of only a little over two miles each way, but we had been so long in the saddle that the march nearly killed some of the boys. The step was something fierce. Each trooper seemed to have a little amble of his own that no persuasion could turn into a marching pace.

January 25, 1915. Were issued bandoliers and mess tins today; also clean palliasses. This afternoon a bunch were put through squad drill, that is, regular recruits drill. The Lord only knows what we will be doing next. I am losing hope of ever getting to the front at all.

January 26, 1915. Was supposed to be a mounted orderly to Maj. Alderson this morning, but unfortunately—for him—I caught a slight cold last night and my face swelling up I went sick and loafed around the house all day. Wore a pair of borrowed slippers and spent a lazy day, only working at mealtimes when I condescended to come to the table.

PREPARATIONS

Instructions were given this afternoon to the RCDs to hold themselves in readiness to move off at a moment's notice. All kit is to be discarded except saddlery, sword, cloak and one pair of extra socks, extra underwear, handkerchiefs, comb and toothbrush.

From now on mounted parades are to be taken part in by all available men in full marching order. Horses carrying full feed bags, etc. We were advised to procure little bags to carry tea or coffee, sugar and flour in. Each section will likely take care of its own cooking. Where we are to go is a mystery, opinion being divided between France and Egypt. At present Cavalry are not being used in either place. It seems queer that we should have our kit reduced to merely what our horses can carry.

The First Batt. are to move to France on Friday 29th. Col. Hill, their O.C., appears on parade each morning as drunk as a fiddle and

Maj. Osborne, of the 24th Gray Horse, also has been hitting up the Joy Fluid pretty hard, and raised such ructions the other morning that the company left the parade ground and went back to their tents until such time as a complaint was attended to.

January 27, 1915. This morning, I put on my disguise, which consists of a dirty, black, civilian overcoat, a muffler crossed in front (true English style), a sloppy peaked cap, and rubber boots. With this outfit, borrowed from our carpenter, I am able to beat my way around very successfully, and avoid questions from officers.

When I first costumed myself in this rigout the boys billeted with me nearly went crazy with laughing. I used it successfully at night but was recognized twice today. After swearing them to secrecy I left them laughing helplessly in the middle of the road and beat it on my way. The boys are going to accompany me to the photographers tonight and I will send you photos.

Had a bath at the Post Office which has the only public bath in town. If I were to tell them that at home we have two bathrooms I would be set down as a second Baron Munchausen.

It may seem funny to make a note of such an apparently unimportant thing as a bath but when you consider that my last one was a week before Xmas and the one before that was early in October, a bath becomes an Occasion. (Many in this contingent have not had a bath since leaving Canada and others will not wash before their return, if they go back.)

January 28, 1915. Preston came home jagged last night and as a consequence he wanted to stay up all night and argue everything from "How much better England was than Canada" to "How many months can a man go without a change of underwear and socks, and still feel clean."

This last subject caused a great deal of discussion on account of the small kit we are to carry away shortly. Gorse stated he once wore a suit for three months, without feeling any the worse for it. Ericsson is going to wear two suits of underwear and socks and give over space in his cloak pockets to tobacco & matches. Charlton plans to rob the dead & loot houses for any changes of clothing he wants. On one point all are unanimous—"Keatings Insect Powder must accompany the troops!!"

Orderly-Room Sgt McCutcheon rode up here yesterday afternoon to get address of my next-of-kin. However, there are several small issues to be given us before they move us to active service: Bank Books to be sewn in lower left hand corner of serge; emergency rations (a packet of bouillon cubes). An identification tag is worn like a scapular. Last and most important, we MUST have rifles and ammunition!

Spent the day on sick list and will try the same gag tomorrow as there is going to be a regimental ride to Pond Farm. I look healthy as a lumberjack, but by putting a plaintive note in my voice, and with the assistance of my comrades-in-arms, who are cheerful liars, I think I can stall another day....

January 30, 1915. Winterburn-Stokes, Wilts. I am billeted with seven others in a large room, which is a sort of wing to a double house. Four of us have meals in one of the houses. I find the meals at the cottage as good if not better than we had in Shrewton. This house is very picturesque with a thatched roof that reminds me of a Buster Brown haircut.

We are all to get black boots in a few days regardless of the fact that many received new pairs only a short time ago. In spite of these preparations the troopers are pessimistic about ever leaving, and some maintain they will not believe it until they are on their way and will doubt it then.

The machine gun Section have been notified that their Colts will be taken from them and Maxims substituted. Colts are good but Maxims better adapted to the service they will be used for. So far, they have been getting their instruction from Detail Handbooks, so you can see that they are in no position to meet an enemy.

THE KING'S VISIT

February 3, 1915. Were inspected this morning at Lark Hill by Gen. Seely, now in command of the Canadian Cavalry—a rehearsal for inspection by King George tomorrow. Lark Hill now looks like a city: huts of wood, tin and canvas cover the Plains, laid out in "streets," numbered one way and lettered the other, with canteens, a moving picture show, laundry, etc. The railway, its siding filled with freight cars, gives the camp a real metropolitan appearance.

The platform from which the King is to review the contingent is a plain wooden affair, three feet from the ground with a wooden railing. A path of sand runs from the stand back to the railway where another small platform has been built.

February 4, 1915. The lilies of the field are not attired as were the Alberta Dragoons today at Lark Hill! They had new Stetson hats, Strathcona boots, Lee-Enfield carbines or rifles (likely rifles as they carried bayonets on the right sides of their belts); swords in dull green sheaths carried on the near side of the saddle.

To our left, huge masses of infantry formed up. I never saw a better display and the King, Lord Kitchener, Gen. Alderson and the rest said they were a fine example of Canadian Militia.

I was much surprised at the way some artillery batteries had their guns and limbers painted. They were daubed all over with splotches of dark red, blue, green and brown paint. I suppose that these are neutral colours at a distance, but at ten or twenty yards they are the most glaring exhibitions you ever saw.

The Special Train steamed in about 10:30, the band in front struck up "God Save the King," the royal standard was raised and Kitchener's artillery perched up on top of a distant hill started firing the customary salute.

For a wonder, the drizzle which had been descending all morning stopped just about this time. "His Machesty" accompanied by a large staff started a personal inspection on foot, walking very slowly.

Then King George, Kitchener and Gen. Alderson took their places in the grandstand, which had the hand rail painted red for the occasion. Gen. Seely took a position of vantage on a lumber pile and slapped his arms vigorously against his body to keep warm. He looked so like a rooster with his red face and cap that I could not resist a laugh. He seems to be a pretty decent head and the cavalry are well satisfied to have him in charge.

Two moving picture operators and a score of photographers were on the grounds.

When the Inspecting Party had taken up its position, we started off at a trot. The parade took two hours to pass. After that we rode up beside the railway for about a mile and a quarter and waited for the train to pull out so that we could give three cheers for the King.

MOVING TROOPS

The Infantry, Artillery, Transports, etc, are leaving for France tomorrow, and by the first of next week all will be gone—except us Cavalry, who have no place to go, apparently.

February 5, 1915. Were told this morning to have all our kit and saddlery ready to leave for the East Coast. The Q.M. has ordered transports to convey stores to Amesbury where we are to entrain. Hope it is true.

Edgar *{brother in Medical Corps in France}* writes that English cavalry are being used in trenches but there is no chance of our being used in a similar manner.

Albert Smith of the Dragoons was offering to bet even money that the RCDs would never be used in the German War, but no-one would take him up, so you can see how gloomy we consider our chances of seeing active service. The kit which belonged to Phillips was sold at public auction. The proceeds were sent to Phillips' people in Canada along with pay which was due him. The boys were disgusted and said they would prefer to have their stuff burned or given away.

The English remark on the independence, or you might call it cheek, of the colonial troops, particularly Canadians who never salute an officer (unless they know him personally); talk back to any who reprimand them and, generally, go about as though they owned the earth. A few days ago a sentry halted a party of soldiers with "Who goes there?" Reply was "A detachment from Ninth Wiltshire Yeomanry." Sentry: "Advance, Wiltshire Yeomanry! All is well." A few minutes later, obliged to halt another bunch, he was told to "Go to Hell." He immediately responded "Advance, Canadians! All is well."

Heard an instructive and elevating debate between Squires of Ottawa and Ruttledge of Toronto, both in this billet. They were in the undertaking business before joining the Drag's and hope to carry on some dark work with the Germans. I know a lot about embalming now.

February 7, 1915. Markess of our transport who has been in hospital, won some money playing poker. This made him feel better so he promptly beat it to London. As soon as he returns they will give him his $8 suit and transportation.

February 8, 1915. The 48th Highlanders have gone and the balance will be marching out for the next few days. Great numbers of Motor Lorries are passing all the time.

The Major put us through mounted drill with rifles and buckets today, followed this up with four charges and subsequent rallies, and then we had an attack on an imaginary advance guard.

Gen. Seely told us that he has written Sir John French that the Royal Canadian Dragoons are ready to take the field. Nevertheless it will be a month before we leave England, I am afraid. We are only one cavalry regiment out of half a dozen in England, but cavalry is not needed at present.

February 9, 1915. Parade today consisted of galloping led horses. We did some very fast work. Finally we were obliged to run about 25 yards, mount and get away at a gallop in twenty seconds—no mean stunt, loaded down with rifle, haversack, waterbottle, bandolier and wearing ammunition boots which feel like snowshoes and look like boats!

Our saddles are constantly in readiness, being packed with overcoat, saddle sheet, mess tin, heelpegs and shackle, hay net, oat bag and sword. A section of built-up headrope is put around the horses' neck and one saddle blanket and two sleeping blankets, under the saddle. This is quite a load, but we pack it away with good system. With all this kit "posting" is next to impossible, so we just sit tight and get jarred stiff at every jump of the horse.

Joe Ruttledge was brought home to our billet by Sgt Bill Dorsey and Fenimore & Lewis. Joe wanted to lick the world but was so paralyzed that he could not move a leg, so was just pitched into a corner where he lay till Reveille.

ELLIOTT'S HORSE

February 10, 1915. You may have noticed reference to a corps from British Columbia known as "Elliott's Horse" who seemed to be wandering at large among the cavalry here. They have been a considerable mystery. Robert Lowe, an ex-Blue, gave me the history, and allowed me to read the statement which follows. There was only three copies printed—one each to the War Office, Mr R.J. Elliott and the one Lowe now holds. The full facts of the case are not yet known in B.C. Capt. Smith was given a commission in King Edward's Horse, but after the War Office saw the facts as printed here, he was cashiered, also the other officer.

The following is a statement of the history of Elliott's Horse of Victoria, B.C. and the reasons for objecting to Capt. A.G.G. Smith as "Officer Commanding." Elliott's Horse was organized in Victoria early in September, 1914. Smith and Underwood who had taken part in raising the Victoria Squadron of the B.C. Horse, but were passed over on officers being appointed to that Corp, induced Mr. R.J. Elliott, K.C. and others to finance a squadron of 80 ex-servicemen to be sent to England. Statements were made to the men offering their services that the squadron would leave for England in a few days; that horses and equipment were already waiting there and that pay at Canadian rates would be allowed for each man from date of joining the squadron till date of actual enlistment.

Each man was asked to and the majority signed an agreement to the effect that he would serve H.M. the King for three years..., and remain with E. Horse or as the War Office should think fit.

A week after the corps was started, our officers told us that, instead of carrying out the original plan, we were...to wait a few days till we could get recognition from the Militia Dept. which would mean pay at Canadian rates and, most important to the married men, Canadian Separation allowance and return to Canada at the close of the war.

After several weeks daily training, Capt. Smith asked all the men to attend a concert at H.Q. at which he would make a clear statement of the situation. This practically amounted to one item: that we never could obtain authorization from the Canadian Government. Several questions were asked and during the discussion, Underwood said that he was forced to tell us that the truth of the matter was that Capt. Smith was our stumbling block—several influential people having refused their support while he was in command. Capt. Smith at once denied this and a general quarrel followed among the officers. The meeting broke up by some of the men leaving in disgust and their spokesman requesting the officers to discuss their affairs in their own quarters.

After this the officers could not be held in any respect so the men took the matter to Mr. Elliott appointing four of their number as representatives.

Three of the officers had handed in their resignations to Capt. Smith. Therefore Mr Elliott asked the men to choose their temporary leaders. The squadron unanimously decided to leave this entirely in Mr. Elliott's hands, upon which the officers patched up their quarrels and decided to go on as before.

Mr Elliott at this time promised to send the squadron as an independent one and arranged for its immediate departure for England.

The squadron eventually left Victoria on the —. Capt. Smith preceding it by a faster route. We travelled to Montreal thence to Glasgow by *Letitia* of Donaldson Line in charge of Underwood. We were met by Capt. Smith who had arranged to have us embodied in King Edwards Horse as a reserve squadron. This suited most of the men, but as there were a number of points referring to pay, leave, married men's allowances and a few smaller items to be talked over, we decided to ask Capt. Smith to go into these at once as we knew that after being attested we would not be in a position to insist on it.

Our first claim was for the dismissal of three of our temporary officers, owing to their disgraceful behaviour on the voyage. We referred Capt. Smith to the officers on the *Letitia* as we were certain the latter would agree that any want of discipline & decency among us was on our officers' part.

This point Capt. Smith listened to, promising we should see no more of the men referred to, but refused point blank to listen to anything further till we were attested, and threatening us with arrest if we refused. His ground for this last was that we had all signed an agreement in Montreal before a notary that we would join whatever corps we were required to. (We did put our names to such a document but only under compulsion—Underwood as acting O.C. in Montreal telling us that if we did not care to sign we need not, but we would have to leave the squadron, turning in whatever kit we had drawn. This meant that we should have been left 3000 miles from either our destination or our homes without means; therefore everyone signed.)

As Capt. Smith continuously refused to discuss matters, our only course was to refuse to take the oath in K.E. Horse and to put ourselves right with the Colonel of the Regiment. We explained to him, through his adjutant, our position. Col. Craddock then gave us until 9 a.m. the following day to swear in or leave barracks and as Capt. Smith still refused to have any inquiry, we appointed temporary N.C.Os, etc. and marched the next day to the Union Jack Club where we remained till we were able to settle our affairs.

Our main grounds of complaint were:

1) After promises made, we had received only $2 pay during the whole trip of over 6000 miles.

2) After similar promises, nothing was being told us about back pay which had amounted to a considerable sum in each case.

3) The married men had been told that in the event of our being required to join an Imperial Service Unit, when a separation allowance would not be enough to keep a family living in B.C., arrangements were to be made with Mr. Elliott to have such families looked after. Nothing had apparently been done about this.

4) A number of smaller points such as the disbursement of money said to have been given by Mr. Elliott and others for use on the trip to England; the reasons of our travelling steerage on a small boat after being told by Mr. Elliott that 2nd class fares were being booked for us.

Most of these items could have been discussed in a very short time, and if any reason whatever had been given by Capt. S. for the non-fulfillment of promises made for us, no doubt all the men would have met him half-way. The married men could not of course have joined an Imperial Unit unless an allowance was made their families to meet with Western conditions. So many false statements had been made that we could not trust a verbal promise.

It is only with the greatest reticence and under compulsion

so that the authorities can hear both sides of this case and do justice to us that we have made the above statement.

It should be added that an unfortunate incident occurred at Hounslow Barracks when we refused to give up to Capt. Smith the Squadron papers including Medical Certificates. We hold that we were entitled to these but Col. Craddock decided they should be left with Capt. Smith. We therefore returned the case intact to Col Craddock.

The undersigned representing the members of "Elliott's Horse" agree that the foregoing is a correct statement of all that took place in connection of the separation of the men of "E.H." from their provisional officers on 17th October, 1914.
W.K. Walker, Act O.C.
H.L. Gracey
F.C. Brewer
L.O. Adams
Robert Lowe—Member Com. and 36 Others on behalf of the men of Elliotts Horse.

Since the corps was disbanded, the majority have joined the RCDs & LSH. Lowe has obtained a commission in the Scottish Horse and is just waiting for his discharge from the RCDs to go to his regiment. Others have received commissions in the English Territorial Army. The men were all from good positions in B.C. and number among them architects, clerks, merchants and ranchers, etc.

ARMS AND EQUIPMENT

February 11, 1915. Rode over to Rolleston and Bustard with the troop for exercise this a.m. Both camps were deserted except for a few workmen. We were allowed to dismount and go in search of whatever might be of use to us. We got heel pegs, tent mallets, shovels, rakes, a wheelbarrow and a lot of blankets. A great number of rifle chests and ammunition boxes were scattered about; some partly full and some may have been full. Certainly, many pounds of equipment went to waste.

February 13, 1915. Got up at 4 a.m. yesterday and rode to Shrewton where we were joined by A & B Squadrons and a few from

C, who helped to make up the complete strength of our troop. At 7:15, we started for Pond Farm where we were joined by a section of R.C.H.A.

The Strathconas were approaching from Upavon and we were to meet and give them battle. The fog was so thick that we could not see men ten horses lengths in front, so several parties on both sides were surprised and captured. (We took a gun section which walked to within twenty yards of us before they knew who we were.) It was an agreeable day and we are to have many more.

Gen. Seely announced today that we would be issued with the Lee-Enfield rifle instead of Rosses, and long buckets instead of short buckets and arm slings. We exchanged our bandoliers for the new type which carries five pockets in front containing cartridges in clips of five.

Our move to Crowborough has been cancelled. We are to go to France in two weeks. (What, again?) However, this rumour seems authentic (as usual) having Gen. Seely as mouthpiece.

The men have been worried since the Brigade has been taken into the Imperial Service for fear we would be given their Pay, which is 28 cents. However their fears were dispelled. It's a lucky thing we are not in the French Army where the rank and file are paid a penny a day and a colonel makes two bits. At present, Belgian soldiers get no pay at all.

February 14, 1915. Was glad to hear Edgar received one of the Queen's Xmas boxes. They were not issued here and are considered as valuable as Queen Victoria's chocolate boxes.

February 15 1915. Winterburn-Stokes, Wilts. We all had an extra bandolier, Oliver belt and Ross bayonet issued yesterday and when the bandoliers are filled with 50 rounds of ball ammunition, they make quite a load to carry around, much more to mount or dismount a horse rapidly with. The bayonet issue and subsequent practice has started a rumour that we are to be used as infantry after all.

We have had several extracts from books read to us lately, dealing with the tactics employed by Germans, etc., also the proper answers to challenges by French sentries, so it looks like a trip to France. The books were sent to squadron & company commanders only, and are considered very confidential. They state that:

—*no churches are to be used at any time for housing of the wounded as* they are not protected from German shell fire by the fact that they are churches.

—Cavalry patrols must always ride with swords at the ready and, on sighting a mounted patrol of the enemy, a charge should be made at once, no matter how superior the Germans are in number as the morale of the Germans is entirely gone.

—The German Uhlans throw down their lances and beat it on the slightest provocation. They do not fight but retreat to where their supports are and endeavour to bring their attackers under fire from trenches where these supports are hidden.

BUFORD RIFLE RANGES

February 18, 1915. Got up at 6 a.m. and, after a hasty breakfast, went to stables and turned out, saddled and equipped, with 50 rounds ball ammunition per man. The ammunition was issued in canvas strips and slung from the shoulder so you can throw the empty container away. Leather bandoliers will now be ornamental dress—like brass helmets.

At 8, we joined the rest of C squadron near Stonehenge and started for Buford Camp Rifle Ranges. We were given five shots each at ten yards, at 100 yards and 200 yards, + disappearing targets and in Rapid Fire. In close trenches an enemy could not glance over his cover before being spotted by a Dragoon—if we shoot like we did today. I did fairly well considering lack of practice.

This was my first visit to Buford, and I was surprised to find it a most artistic and permanent-looking camp. Hundreds of wooden huts lined the sides of well built streets. The roofs were painted green and the sides red. The brick Post Office would do credit to many good sized towns and neat terra cotta houses stood along the main road, no doubt intended for Staff. The streets and houses were well lit with electric arc lamps and many huts had telephones, to judge by the number of wires strung from the poles. A Wesleyan chapel, moving picture theatre, hospital, also a large building with a sign ("Miss Perks Home for Soldiers") were some notable buildings we passed.

Near the ranges we ran on new huts some with workmen still on them. You might call these the suburbs. The houses were a dirty lead colour and the streets were mud of the best English variety. The streets are called after London thoroughfares such as Oxford Street, Park Lane, etc.

We started back in a rainstorm, which changed to such violent hail that we were obliged for a time to turn our horses' backs to it and huddle by the roadside. Just before Amesbury, the storm cleared up and we enjoyed a fast trip home.

We are short three horses in this troop and some men must beg or borrow a horse to take part in a parade. I am lucky to get a good mount, #240 which I call Polly. The only other name I know for a horse is George!

LIFE IN CAMP

February 19, 1915. 8 p.m. Today Germany starts to make good her bluff of blockading the British Isles to starvation. I think a spell of starvation would do the RCDs good. We look quite aldermanic as we struggle to climb aboard a horse.

Some of our men whose homes are in England were saying that when they visit, they put on clean clothes instead of the muddy uniform they had been wearing on the plains, but their friends insist that they get back into uniform. Lowe's father was indignant at his want of good taste & common sense in visiting his home in mufti.

Healthy young men are positively despised in some places if they are not in khaki and clerks make a point of telling customers in an embarrassed manner their very good reasons for not being in the Army. It is not uncommon for a waitress (or some other person not eligible for enlistment themselves!) to make audible remarks about young men in mufti whom they never saw before but think should be wearing khaki.

February 21, 1915. Paraded sick to Dr. Todd this morning for to get a three-day pass to Salisbury to see a dentist. My teeth are not bad and I have kept care of them but I thought it better to have them looked over before leaving England.

Went to the English Church here tonight. The church is very similar to an R.C. with altar, candelabra and a baptismal fount where we have holy water founts. Their service also was similar, except they left out a great deal of ritual including the most important part—Taking Up The Collection. They take the collection on the First Sunday of every month, when they also give communion, so you get something for your money.

This morning, Joe Ruttledge from Toronto, was had up for going to sleep on picket. He was fined three pounds. Stratton was fined five pounds fifteen shillings for being drunk on duty. This is a new idea of heavily fining soldiers for misdemeanours instead of plain C.B. or extra fatigues. It has been found that nothing straightens a man up like a punch in the pocket book, and a good, hearty wallop every time.

February 22, 1915. Bell of the 4th Troop died yesterday. He was from the E.H. and leaves a small ranch which he had just got into good shape by very hard work, in the West. He is to be buried with full honours by the 4th Troop, with the luxury of a nice little casket and wreath of flowers—which is more than some of his pall bearers will get in the near future.

February 24, 1915. The remark "Swearing like a trooper" is not without some truth in it. To hear a cavalryman at his best, catch him saddling in the rain or snow or in the dark, particularly if his mount is restive. The last few days after range firing, we saddled up in a sleet storm & the collective language on any occasion would furnish a book the size of the dictionary (unabridged). Tug Wilson (reformed since his marriage) contents himself with singing "Jesus loves me, Yes I know; So does Ragtime Cowboy Joe."

We were informed last night that we will move to huts in Crowborough on Monday. We are not at all pleased to give up these comfortable quarters for huts and rations again, much as we like moving around.

There is a dance tonight in the granary of Carey Cole's barn here, given by the RCDs. The 2d Troop are bringing young ladies from Shrewton, Devizes and other places around so that there will be lots of partners. The admission is eighteen pence and includes refreshments. I am not going. My shoes are of the real English hobnail variety—two sizes too big. Moreover I have considerable of a rip in the rear of my khaki riding breeches, my Bedford cords being also at the tailors to be patched.

February 27, 1915. Am having breakfast in tea rooms in St. Thomas' Square. This city has suffered most appallingly in the numbers of her young men who have fallen at the front; but they are not nearly so bad as the London Guards & Household Troops which have been brought down from entire regiments to a handful. The Household Cavalry has lost seven men out of eight.

Met a sergeant from a B.C. regiment tonight. He had just returned from a holiday on the firing line in France. He had been granted a ten-day pass here, and went to visit friends in the trenches!! He says the work has become a routine and men crawl around in the trenches on their hands and knees, visiting their friends just the same as you would walk across the road.

Both sides are so entrenched that it seems impossible for either side to advance. Everything is covered with vermin and when the troops leave the trenches after a few days the first thing they do is to change their clothes but the change is no better than what they just discarded.

There is a jolly crowd here at the "Y" & the place is filled with soldiers. The only drawback is that about 9 p.m. the secretary comes into the smoking room and asks or begs of you with a most tearful voice to attend prayers upstairs. "It won't take a second longer than ten minutes, old chap. Better come." "Naw! I don't wanna get saved. Got saved once tonight; they put me out of the Haunch of Venison before I had a chance to get a skinful."

The B.C. Sgt was saying that when the English soldiers wanted to practice some hot shooting, one of them yelled toward the enemy lines "Waiter! Waiter!" and immediately a half dozen Huns, taken by surprise, would pop their heads above the trenches' top.

9 p.m. Winterburn-Stokes. We're to leave for an unknown destination on Tuesday at 8, but would not be surprised if we went to a port and took a troop ship for the continent.

March 1, 1915. Muir was on guard today and his duties carried him too many times to The Bell but we managed to keep him out of sight. I packed his saddle and got his horse groomed for him.

This morning's exercise took us over the downs past a fine golf links & private clubhouse. The downs are studded with training courses with jumps, both ditches and hurdles. We are asked to keep off these "Gallops" as much as possible.

9 p.m. Got a ride back from Shrewton with a labourer. He was well soused and drove down hills and around corners at a dead gallop to get here before the pub closed. I was near dead with fright.

The Bell was filled with soldiers & farmers and they were all lit up like cathedrals to celebrate the leavetaking of the Dragoons. Two men at the door were forcibly helped into their coats, but, outside of that, there was no unpleasantness. Everybody leaned up against the nearest stationary object and looked about with vacant and happy expressions on their faces.

In one room an impromptu program was in progress. A bearded shepherd called "Golden Slippers" after the song he sings on the slightest provocation—say two pots of ale—was engaged in his regular song & dance number and the audience joined the chorus. He skipped about in his heavy brogans in a style that would do justice to shepherds in a comic opera. He gave way to a young farmer who sang "My Little Gray Home in the West" very well and could not have done any better if he was sober.

At 8:05 p.m. the bell rang and the concert finished in the street. Hopkins was very amusing. He put a tin pail without a bottom over his head and, with the handle behind his neck, wore it like a dog's muzzle. He thought he was a submarine.

March 2, 1915. We are not leaving until 9 a.m. so Lefurgy was sent to tell the night picket, and (feeling very happy) he thought he would batter down their door with rocks. Ralph, Squires and Ruttledge thought the Germans were bombing them and were scared stiff. Ruttledge poked his sword out of a crack in the door and wiggled it frantically to head off an attack, while the other two rattled their knees together and their hair stood perfectly upright.

Libby & Wilson could not put in an appearance at afternoon stables; we got an alibi for Libby by answering to his name at roll call, but Wilson was simply excused as being drunk. There will be another celebration tonight as now we do not leave until 9 a.m.

MARESFIELD CAMP

March 4, 1915. Maresfield Camp, Sussex. After all that secrecy they have landed us here: 41 miles east of London—where we had an idea we were going to war.

On our arrival, Terrien, McKean and myself were sent to guard the baggage. It was so cold and miserable that I took refuge inside a contractor's shanty near the track. I crawled through the window and discovered some blankets on the floor. It did not take me long to roll myself in these and when I awoke it was 4 a.m., the train bearing the Second Troop, horses and baggage was gone and the last train just about to leave. I crawled aboard and slept again until we landed in Buxted at about nine o'clock.

The other troops started to unload horses, etc., but I beat it and walked into camp after having breakfast at a Wheelmaker's Inn. I arrived just in time for dinner and found my kit looked after, my horse and saddle put away by the other men in my section. I had no difficulty in excusing my absence; they did not know but what I had helped load the cars in Amesbury.

We are now in huts and I find them very comfortable and roomy. Each man had trestles on which to lay three boards for a bed and palliasse. Two long tables are used for dining, reading & writing. A stove stands at each end of the room and there are large windows. Our horses are in sheds with concrete floors, electric lights and fine feed troughs, about 200 yards from the huts.

Cinder paths are just being completed. It has been very wet here but the soil is sandy.

The camp was the property of Prince Munster, a German who left for home (where he now is in the Army) shortly before the war. It was then discovered he was the head of espionage here in England and his estates were confiscated by the Government. No doubt the Prince thought he would be back here entertaining the Kaiser by this time.

Maresfield, outside the gate, is a church, three or four stores, blacksmith shop and The Chequers Inn.

March 5, 1915. Took my Bedford breeches to a tailor in Uckfield, a town about two miles from here. They are a pair I got from the 1st Hussars and better than what we are issued.

Happening to go into The Bell we found a very good if rough house concert underway. The Pubs are under instructions not to sell "spiritous liquor" to any of the troops but there is no ban on beer, port or stout. The rule was not in force until the Canadians arrived.

Two buses like Dietches' sightseeing cars run between the town and camp and the fare was 4d but on arrival of the colonials the drivers tried to raise the price. We are pretty tired of this sort of robbery and so tonight the soldiers insisted on being driven into Maresfield for the regular price—or they would wreck the car. Four pence is the established price now.

We got in after lights out but as our road is not past the Guard we can practically come and go as we please.

The Strathconas have a special guardhouse for their men. At present 40 men await trial for drunkenness. When the regiment left Pewsey, they had to send fatigue parties with wheelbarrows to their billets after the absentees.

March 6, 1915. We are getting rations on a new system. A mess orderly is appointed each night for the following day. Breakfast consists of bacon or sausage, bread, jam, tea or coffee. Sometimes you cannot tell the difference. Also porridge, without milk or sugar, generally burned.

For dinner: steak or chops, hash or stew, boiled potatoes. For supper—jam, bread, cheese and pressed meat. Tea for all meals.

This is luxury compared to Pond Farm and better than we got at Val Cartier yet some are always grousing about service rations.

BRIGADE POLICEMAN

March 8, 1915. Uckfield Station, Uckfield, Sussex. About two o'clock, I walked into Uckfield and my duties were very general: simply to see that any soldiers I might run across were behaving themselves. Quite a snap. I liked this job and when I said so on my return, Berteau put me on Brigade Police permanently. So I am now practically off the Regimental Strength and attached to Brigade H.Q. I am tickled to death. When the other fellows answer the Reveille trumpet, I just turn over until as late as 8 o'clock. We do not pay on the bus. At the Cinema the police are admitted free. We answer no roll calls or parades, and are excused from pickets, guards and fatigues.

Of course everything is not fixed up for us yet. Sgt Foster is going to get us a room in Headquarters and we will have meals cooked by the H.Q. chef (*Chef*, mind you—not cook!) This position is permanent and we follow the Brigade as Policemen from now on.

I am much obliged for Mother's offer to send me fruit cake but I can buy all such things here. At Xmas, foolish hampers were sent to the Canadians. One of our men had two dressed chickens sent from Alberta and when they arrived, the poor chickens were blue! I have never gone hungry since I joined. Some of the meals have been bad, but I always had money enough to buy a meal or enough grub to satisfy my appetite.

March 15, 1915. While in the bakeshop yesterday afternoon, I met the wife of Sgt Calloway of the RCDs. She said my face was familiar and wanted to know if I was from Stanley Barracks. Mrs. Calloway is quite slangy and breezy and talks, talks and talks. These wives who follow their soldier husbands about remind me of the wives of the jockeys. They know all about the men in their favourite regiments, and the familiar cap badge is sufficient introduction for them, provided your face is clean.

March 23, 1915. Maresfield Park, Sussex. Had supper at the Holly Bush Tavern. After, I went to the cinema. Added attractions: "Marseillaise" was sung by a French Canadian RCHA, going through all the dramatic poses and using his hands freely. An LSH Trooper sang "Thora" very well and Star Performer Miss Artye Couche (get the spelling!) sang patriotic songs calculated to keep the Canadians happy. She sang "Your King & Country Need You," "Tommy, Lad" and "My Little Gray Home in the West." This last is very popular with the Canucks.

The batteries have a lot of talent including the son of Houdini, the handcuff king. He is almost as good as his father and gives exhibitions in Uckfield, getting out of straight jackets, handcuffs or as many coils of rope as you can find places on him to tie it. He does some dancing while tied in the straight jacket and "The Drunkard's Reel" wins great applause when he falls down apparently from too much Red Eye and keeps time with his head, hands and heels on the floor.

A gunner from "A" Battery, RCHA, says that he is disgusted with the artillery. He said their horses were so soft that he did not think them capable of pulling the guns and limbers from Winchester to Southampton, an order we expect some of these days. He also told me that he has had only had three drills on the gun, in Pointing, etc., and has forgotten half of the necessary detail; some gunners have forgotten it all.

March 24, 1915. This morning, Capt. Doherty detailed me to walk through the lines and drive out all civilians, hucksters, photographers, etc., without passes. Little boys come into the Park every evening and I will have to shoot a half dozen or so tonight, as an example.

So far I have kicked out two little girls and a boy in a dog cart; three hucksters, one of whom was lame and unable to run as fast as the others; one newspaper vendor; and three waggons. I have become a desperate man, and after we get revolvers I will be unbearable.

2:40 p.m. Michael Kelly of "A" Squadron, RCDs had his court martial sentence read out before the regiment this noon. He was asleep on sentry go and during active service. All he got was 54 days C.B. In 1850 he would have been shot without much deliberation.

MARCHING ORDERS

March 26, 1915. All was excitement here this afternoon. At 1:30 Sgt Doyle came in with orders for everyone to be ready to move at a moment's notice & to have kits packed for the transports. I could hear the Strathconas cheering like mad and the RCHA were already forming on their parade ground.

All these preparations made me fear that the entire brigade would go to Southampton to embark, leaving us practically homeless. As a committee of one, I approached the Brigade Orderly Clerk Norman of the RCDs and he stated that *he* would let us know when they were *really* going to leave.

However, nearly everyone was positive they were leaving for good. I even saw a cook out of the 2nd KEH gallop back, after the regiment was moving off, for a pair of riding breeches he had forgotten, and come back with them hanging around the horse's neck.

The marching order was received at 1:45 p.m. and the whole brigade was on the road by 3:30 which is very good time for 2,150 men and horses but they came back about 5:30, having only gone about a mile on the other side of Buxted.

After supper I walked to the Chequers Inn where Robby was supposed to be on duty. But Robby was not there. It seems he had bet two bob on the Grand National and when Ally Sloper galloped home, Robby was made the possessor of five quid; two or three bottles of Johnny Walker did the rest.

When the getaway order was given out at noon, he was so exhilarated that he took his horse from the stables, led it over to his hut and proceeded to give it a thorough grooming in the middle of the room, afterward permitting it to drink out of the men's water pail. However, before he could saddle it, some interfering NCO accompanied by the guard came along and put Robby forcibly to bed.

Heard tonight that seven German cruisers had slipped past the English fleet from the Kiel canal and that this brigade are liable to get many such marching orders as they had today, as we are only eighteen miles from Brighton which has a long pier suitable for the landing of soldiers in boats or small cruisers. While there is nothing there worth taking, the Germans would like to make a demonstration in Great Britain to hearten up their countrymen. So it is up to the First Canadian Mounted Brigade to be able to move quickly to repel a land attack. This, of course, is merely a theory which the men have got hold of. It may be only a practice turnout, but the orders are supposed to have come suddenly from the War Office.

March 27, 1915. Another marching order was given this a.m. at 4:30. They were ready to march off at 6:30 when ordered to return the horses to the stables. An hour later they were on the road again but about noon the RGAs returned to camp.

March 28, 1915. Bitterly cold last night. Sgt Foster asked me this morning if I would like the day off. He said I had been pretty steady on the Park & had been working hard. Haw! Haw! I had to look hard at him to see if he was joking, but he evidently meant it, so I told him I would prefer to wait until Payday, and then take a couple of days.

I was made a present of a real good Havana cigar from America and it put me in mind of my Sunday evening strolls up Woodward Avenue. Cigars here make fierce smokes unless you pay a high price for them. A "Marcella" (5 for a shilling) smells like a livery stable and tastes worse.

I often come in for such little handouts—part of a policeman's graft! At the SPD shop I get a threepenny reduction on the price of a meal. At the Daily House I am often pressed to take two mugs of milk for the price of one.

March 29, 1915. Accompanied by Tracy I walked into Fairwarp last night. Tracy was in Chile when war was declared and with about 40 others was secretly drilling in a Young Men's English Club there. He and four others intended to take the first steamship leaving Valparaiso for England and were hanging about the docks when the German fleet entered and Admiral Von Spee announced in great glee that he had sunk the English ships *Good Hope* and *Monmouth*. The English passenger boat was tied up indefinitely so the five of them crossed the Andes mountains—a feat very rare and dangerous.

They arrived before Xmas and the War Office sent them here. The 2nd KEH is a permanent cavalry regiment raised since war started; recruits sign on for three years (Win, Lose or Draw). (After the war the KEH will lose practically all their men by desertion.)

Every colonial who could ride and shoot was sent to the KEH and, when it was announced that every British soldier who could speak foreign languages (so could be used as an interpreter) would receive a bonus of 6d per day, the 2nd KEH stepped out as one man and demanded the bonus. Unfortunately, the languages had to be French, Belgian or German, and these men knew Chinese, Malay, Hindustani, Spanish & Fijian dialects, etc.

New remounts are expected; we hope they will be better than the bunch received by the 2nd KEH. Some of their horses pull up short in the midst of a squadron drill—if anyone hollers "Milk."

March 31, 1915. Sgt Foster told us last night that the troops here were liable to suddenly be called out after April 3rd, and marched off for good, but we police are to take our stuff to the Main Guard House and await orders. This looks like business.

We have turned our swords in to be painted or dipped and will no longer have to keep them polished. Heavy underwear was served to each man and deficiencies in their kits are to be made good at once. All furloughs are stopped and the canteens have been ordered to stock up no more than is required from day to day.

But from past performances you can dope this out: that we are either going to leave shortly, or some time in the far future. We have all given up trying to guess.

April 4, 1915. Maresfield Park. Easter Sunday. Rumour sets the date of our departure at April 10th, but fails to state what year....

April 5, 1915. Nuttley has 50 men for the RFA billeted there until, training completed, they are shipped out to be shot—and a new crew takes their place. They should call the RFA the "Get Out and Go Under Club:" they "Get Out" to the front, and then they "Go Under." I remember one Canadian who could not stand the hardships of Salisbury so, one Monday morning, he deserted to a battery of RFA who were just leaving. On Friday he was back, but this time he only had one leg. No doubt he now has a lucrative position somewhere, knitting socks or painting china plates.

April 8, 1915. A rumour is about that we leave on Saturday, and our SSM spoke to me today about seeing that my saddlery was all in order. I told him that I had been ordered to report to Brigade HQ, but would see to the saddlery anyhow.

I received an issue of puttees, serge and cap at noon. What I need most is riding breeches; I have two pair, but one is badly damaged in front, and the other in rear, so unless I put both pair on I am not properly dressed.

April 11, 1915. I hear that the Canadian Infantry in France, including the First Ontario Battalion, have another severe casualty list, while regulars in England are attacked by nothing more than a cold.

PAYDAY

April 12, 1915. Maresfield Park Sussex. We were paid on Saturday. The Paymaster did not have enough money to go round. I still have two pounds coming to me.

The Paymaster does the troops out of twenty cents on every five dollars, as they give us a pound ($4.80) but charge us as having received $5.00. Something should be done about this, as it means enormous graft on the large amounts being handled. The men are afraid to go to the Colonel as, for all we know, he may be in on the deal. When we go to France or Turkey the authorities may further fix the exchange and rake in half a dollar or more on every five we get.

April 14, 1915. Uckfield and other important towns near the coast now turn off their street lights early in the evening, and blinds are shut so as to exude as little light as possible to guard against a Zeppelin raid, thought to be threatening the coast.

April 15, 1915. This morning the troops returned from drill about 11. At noon, word came that they were to be ready to leave. I think it is just practice, occasioned by the Zeppelin raids last night at Blythe; the War Office wants to see how quickly our troops can get under way.

Hartfield, Sussex. Anchor Inn 7:15 p.m. The country hereabouts is nearly all gorse, bracken and some pine woods. I understand that the ground is good and fine crops could be raised, but it is the entailed estate of lords who could not sell their property even if they wished to and they refuse to let it, so thousands of acres lie idle while the poor emigrate to the colonies.

April 16, 1915. Maresfield Park. When I left camp yesterday, the Brigade was still standing to, ready to move, quite sure that they were having their last sight of England.

When I arrived at 11, I was glad to find everyone still here although the 2nd troop went to bed fully dressed, expecting to be called out at any minute. All passes have been stopped indefinitely and trains are bringing back soldiers who received telegrams to rejoin their regiments.

This afternoon I made a capture on the lake of an artilleryman but, after confiscating his fishing tackle, I let him go. He had a hook made out of a bent shingle nail, and his line was a length of yarn taken likely from an old sock. I was almost sorry to deprive him of it after I saw what it was as he could not possibly have caught even a minnow and the idea that he was fishing may have given him some pleasure.

April 17, 1915. 8:30 p.m. YMCA Maresfield Park. The troops do little but take rough exercise rides near camp; word is always left just where they are going, so that they may be recalled quickly. I do not know what the idea is, unless it is that an airship raid may be followed up by a bombardment from sea, and a German landing party sent to do as much damage as possible in a short time and then retire to the ships.

April 19, 1915. Maresfield Park After having a hot bath at noon today, while the rest of the squadron were having an inspection of rifles, swords and bayonets, I saddled up No. 60 and rode to Fairwarp and back. Everybody in camp was busy outside. The Dragoons had an inspection of arms and musketry exercises. The Strathconas were doing musketry or semaphore signal practice. The King Eds were having sword exercises and the Garrison Artillery had a dummy set up on a sort of gallows and the men rode at the figure and tried to thrust it through the heart.

About 3, a battalion of rifles from London with a brass band went through bound for Crowborough. They were nearly all old, and the marching was beginning to tell on them, as it is very warm. I felt beautifully clean and cool after my midday bath and, as I passed and gave the foot sloggers a haughty smile, I came in for some good humoured, envious remarks like pedestrians make when the local millionaire sails by in his Ford.

FALSE ALARMS

April 21, 1915. Five Ash Down—Recreation Room. 6:30 p.m. All the country round here except Maresfield is out of bounds for soldiers until the State of Vigilance is over or we are marched away. You see we live in the midst of alarms—False Alarms!

The last air raid on Blythe and the neighbouring countryside caused two deaths, the victims being: One Hen + One Blackbird = Two Birds, proof that the old saying about killing "Twa' drakes wi' one rock" is a myth.

April 22, 1915. The nights remain very cold. Libby had his blankets stolen shortly after his arrival, and the poor sucker had been sleeping under half a blanket and an overcoat. When I found out, I immediately went over to B Squadron and pinched two blankets for him. Am a genius at this sort of work now. I am never short of anything—for very long.

April 23, 1915. I went into Fairwarp and discovered representatives of every unit in the Brigade in the taproom of the Forester's Arms. The troops were on manoeuvres, and it now has become a habit for the scouting and patrolling parties of both White and Red forces to "lose" themselves and rendezvous at the nearest pub, where they make merry—while their officers wonder "Where have those confounded scouts lost themselves now?"

The percentage of drunkenness (among our troop at least) is higher now than I have ever seen before. It is not uncommon for strangers from other regiments to bring one of our men in, and ask what bed he sleeps in. After which they put him to bed and depart without a word. I have seen as many as three or four carried in on one night.

April 26, 1915. The men are tired of the present inaction especially on account of the Canadian Infantry's good work at Ypres while our Corps (supposedly regular forces) are idle in England. When the casualty list is published, their martial ardour may cool.

In a hundred days the war will have lasted a year. Whether we see Peace or not at the end, it will be a terrible hundred days as both sides are taking up the offensive again.

April 29, 1915. Got my new serge out of the tailor's last night, and now look presentable even without my greatcoat.

I made the acquaintance yesterday of a fellow RCD named C— who lived on Bruce Avenue. C— says he has often seen me but was not sure of me here as I am wearing a moustache, and he did not like to speak to me. At present he is in the guardhouse awaiting sentence for some "crime" or other. (You need not mention this to his people.) He said he thought that there were other Windsorites in the RCDs. I looked around, and sure enough, there in the corner was Grew, the ex-employee of the button factory, reclining gracefully with the butt of a fag in his mouth. And in the opposite corner, sat Clare of Detroit. I made all three acquainted. (Do not use this guardhouse information, as it might be made serious for me as well as rotten for the gentlemen incarcerated.)

ORDERS AT LAST

April 30, 1915. Gen. Seely returned from London yesterday noon. At 2 p.m., all units were warned that we are to leave for France on Monday. Only the RCHA will take their horses. (The second KEH has [already] been informed that they were to go to the front as Infantry.) The Brigade will strengthen the Canadians at Ypres for a few weeks, then either return for our horses or have them sent on. Many are unwilling to go as Infantry, afraid that once in action, we will remain in that capacity until the close of the war.

3:30 p.m. The regiment turned in their Ross rifles and bayonets last night and were issued short Lee Enfields with long bayonets. All saddles are being packed up, and one man out every seven or eight is detailed to remain behind to look after the horses. The farriers are to be left, and Lieut. Broome will look after C squadron at the base here. His men are delighted to leave him behind.

Our swords are being put up in bundles, and will be sent to us with the horses—if we ever see *them* again.

While the majority say they are very keen on going to the front, it was easy to get volunteers to remain in Sussex as grooms until the Regiment is mounted again; some, who were most enthusiastic a month or so ago, were actually pale before their services were accepted! (Of course, men like Alex Wilkinson have wives here, but the others just have cold feet.)

It is improbable that we will immediately go into the firing line. I believe the policy is to place fresh regiments at the base, and gradually work them up to the firing line so that, by the time they reach the front, they are seasoned and acclimatized.

Hundreds of telegrams were sent away yesterday by the men announcing their intended departure. In response there was a large gathering in camp, principally of women and girls coming to bid a possibly Last Farewell to their...heroes?

A bunch of undesirables were led away from our lines this morning. They go to London to receive their shilling, $8 suit and ticket home. Besides Grew of this squadron, there was also young Cooke who returns to Simcoe. Some squadrons returned as many as six!

May 1, 1915. Last night, I went to our squadron QMS and drew rifle, bayonet, two pair breeches, shoes, etc.—enough to equip a man twice. We are to have a full kit bag sent to the base and, as our chances of seeing it again are pretty small, we are advised to carry everything we possibly can.

The new Order is that *everyone is to go;* the men that were to have stayed with the horses now must either go with us—or desert.

Dr. Todd, regimental physician, gave the entire regiment a cursory examination this morning. He merely passed down the room and looked at each man who stood naked beside his bed.

I was just saying how lucky I was to get out of it, when Sgt Foster informed us that the Police had to undergo a physical by Dr. Carr of the Field Army. That exam was just as stiff as when we joined up at Val Cartier. He had no marks against me except that I am hog fat and flabby for want of exercise. Footslogging may take us all down a bit. Everyone is complaining about the weight they have taken on, so you can see we are not very downhearted.

May 2, 1915. Craven put my outfit together at noon, and it's some job! Reminds me of setting up a stove. There are more straps, buckles and odds & ends of tackle than you can count. The knapsack, water bottles, haversack, bayonet and entrenching tools are all fastened in one piece to the belt. In addition there are six cartridge pockets in front each holding 150 rounds of ball ammunition, and the whole outfit is put on like a coat, and fastened with one buckle.

It certainly is a complete rigout and, when packed, so evenly balanced that it is easy to carry. I dispensed with my 45 Colt revolver as being too clumsy with the outfit.

I am at a loss to know just what is expected of Brigade Police at the front, and asked Sgt. Foster if we will go into the trenches. He seemed quite shocked and I even fancied he went pale; he said that we may do funny things, but never anything so foolish as to go anyplace where we are liable to get our blocks knocked off! So I am left with the impression that we are non-combatants. If this is so, I will continue to do my duty cheerfully, but you must not advertise the fact.

May 3, 1915. The three dismounted Cavalry Regiments paraded this afternoon, loaded down and ready to take the road. The 2nd KEH still wore spurs but, outside of that, they looked just like any ordinary infantry brigade, numbering about 2000 in all.

May 4, 1915. Police paraded at 1:15 in marching order. After being looked over by Capt. Doherty, we were told to stay close to HQ, and be ready to move off at 5 p.m.

The regiments must be ready at that time too. The men are allowed one blanket, which they carry, and personal belongings in their knapsacks. No kit will follow them, so they are confident of returning to Maresfield, and getting their horses again.

Bucksted Station 6:40 p.m. We HQ Staff are now in the train, having come by auto with our luggage. We passed the RCDs on the road. They had walked only about a mile and a half but were very tired looking, with the heavy packs they carried. Col. Nelles appeared exhausted but marched the whole way with his load. The Officers carry the same weight as the men and you can hardly tell them apart. We are travelling in comfort as our equipment is in the luggage car while the troopers have their rifles and kit with them.

7:20 p.m. Tunbridge Wells. Anderson, a former welterweight, is in a half pickled state. He has a cartridge in his pocket; on it is carved the name of a certain Sgt Brown of the LSH. However he has a lot of competition for Mr Brown's scalp, and Anderson is afraid he will be beaten in the race for first honours! (I am strictly Temperance!)

We expect to take a ship from Folkestone and land at Bordeaux, France.

{One book is missing here.}

Active Service with Canadian Forces

IN BIVOUAC

May ?, 1915. 6:20 p.m. France. It is very quiet here tonight, no cannon booming, not even an airplane battle. The weather continues good. The Nord Railroad runs a few hundred yards below us and the wounded are taken through daily on Red Cross trains.

I went down to Merriss this morning to get my pay, but was unsuccessful as the paymaster is a very...uncertain individual. I paid a visit to their very fine church. Masons are working on the belltower where the Germans had ensconced their machine guns. The ceiling is riddled with shot, also the walls above the altar. Several stone pillars have been badly chopped up, but are now repaired with cement and "1914" neatly painted over the patch. No chairs or statues have been harmed: the Germans had not yet started on their church pillaging tactics when they occupied this one.

I went back after dinner and received my pay—only fifteen francs (three dollars) twice a month. The 2nd KEH get five francs!

I have practically nothing to do but visit the pubs and see that they close at 8. Sometimes I make a bluff at stopping autos exceeding the ten-mile-an-hour speed limit. My duties, you can see, are simple (even monotonous) not that I would prefer sweating on a route march!

Ten men from each regiment started today to learn the art of setting up barbed wire entanglements. There are two kinds: one is put on permanent posts stuck in the ground, and the other, on long trestles attached together across those trenches or roads which need to be blocked.

A bomb-throwing school is to be started, too. There is quite an art to this, as the fuse has to be timed to the second to make a good cast and then they are thrown 10-20 yards by hand, or farther by means of catapults, slings or throwing sticks. The bomb is about the same size and shape as a can of Gillett's Lye, and two wires (to which the fuse is set) stick out of the top. It is filled with explosive and odd bits of iron scrap and when it explodes (which may cover a radius of twenty feet) it leaves sad memories with the recipient! If it explodes before it is thrown, or close to the bomb throwers' dugout, then the donator is the sorry person.

Stretcher bearers from each group were detailed before we left Maresfield Park. Dr. Todd said they would be better off without the Red Cross on their arms.

May, 1915. Ascension Thursday. This morning, I went to Bailleul with George Mattie, the LSH interpreter. He speaks five languages, and has spent a great part of his life in loafing around like an English younger son. Mattie thinks I am a trifle above the rest of this gang because we are both Catholics!

5:30 p.m. Steemwick. Was detailed to come in here with H.Q. transport and draw our stores and rations. I carried a Lee-Enfield and tried to look like an armed guard! Each driver has a rifle and 300 rounds of ammunition, but I only carry five rounds, trusting to use some of theirs in a pinch. (I do not see how the enemy could get this far back of our trenches, and he would be afraid to fire except at a lonely sentinel.)

I had supper in an estaminet in Belleuil tonight. You go out to the grocer's or butcher's, purchase what you want and the lady cooks it for you. I bought two lamb chops for 16¢ and they were served with bread and coffee for 6¢. The same supper would have cost 35¢ in Detroit. The cafe is well patronized by our "Highlanders," many of whom speak Canadian French very well.

We do not leave for Outersteene until tomorrow morning. The men bivouac in the field with the horses. The word "bivouac" implies that you have the stars for your roof, but I have a tent about 28 inches high set up on a couple of stalks. This is the tent that my predecessors occupied, and so has come to be looked upon as The Police Billet.

Mattie has been censoring letters and he told me of one which ran something like this:

> Dear Father. I am writing this from the trenches. We have been here some time and I am getting fed up with this awful life. The shells are bursting around us something fierce and many of us are dead already. I may be dead before you get this....

In fact, a whole string of lies! Mattie, who is very serious, wrote under this: *This story is a fabrication! Sgt Mattie, LSH censor.*

(Whenever you run across one of these weeping letters you want to look wise, as boys who never heard a shot fired are the best at blood-curdling yarns.)

We get the London papers almost every day. We were not surprised to hear that President Wilson was backing down on the loss of the *Lusitania*. The Canadians and Yanks in this regiment size up the problem in a few words: "The USA has no guts."

LIVING CONDITIONS

I must say for myself that I could not live any better in this country if we were at peace, and I were paying my own way. I've come to look upon myself as a rather expensive luxury supported by the Canadian government. Anyhow, I have the satisfaction of knowing that I am "doing my bit" as they term it in England, and that if *I* were not doing this job, another man would have to do it.

May 14, 1915. I still have a terrible time with the currency here. I have learned to count in French, and know the value of a coin (if you do not hurry me) but when I tender a five-franc note, the change is given in a mixture of English, French and Belgian money which is most confusing, especially the franc and shilling which look alike but have different values. Some Belgian coins are the same size and shape as Yankee nickels, except for a hole in the middle. Then the storekeeper counts the change rapidly on the counter from one side to the other, with a look on his face like a shell game artist.

It rained hard last night and there was heavy firing. I had no ground sheets or blanket, but managed to pinch a few empty sacks and a dirty, slimy, stinking horse blanket; my overcoat made a good covering and I slept very well.

This country is flat, like Essex County. A farmer in the RCDs told me he never saw better farming or pasturing land and Reid has been all over America and England. They raise at least two crops a year, and the barns are large and good. Many houses have thatched roofs, but most are tiled; the insides are clean; some of the exteriors are whitewashed, but the yards and stables are in a most filthy condition.

All water for consumption by our troops is supposed to be purified but this is not always done. Chloride of Lime gives water a horrible medicinal taste and does not quench the thirst in the slightest.

6 p.m. We leave here in a few hours for the first line of billets behind the last line of trenches. I do not know whether we will ride up on the London motor buses, or walk. We have no idea what part of the line we will reinforce, but we will not go into the first line for a few days yet.

Sgt Foster and Sgt Morand seem to have temporarily lost their nerve, and have been trying to strengthen each other with kind words. Foster said "Remember, Morand, if you go under, your wife will get ten dollars a week from the government." Morand made no reply, but his face turned a beautiful yellowish green.

8:15 p.m. The 7th Battalion, Canadian Infantry, has just marched by without any undue noise such as a militia crush makes when they leave Windsor for Camp in Goderich or London. There is quite a difference between untrained men going on manoeuvres and trained men going into action!

CLOSER TO THE FRONT

May 15, 1915. St. Venant. Left Outersteene about 9:30 yesterday. The HQ Staff marched behind Gen. Seely, followed by the LSH, 2nd KEH, RCDs and, in the rear, an immense string of transports, waggons, limbers, field kitchens, packhorses and mules for the ammunition, water detail, etc. In addition, we will likely have motor or horse-drawn ambulances attached to us. (It is marvellous what goes to make up a column going to the front.)

When the head of a column halts for ten minutes, it takes nearly that long for the rest to halt, and by the time the front have moved on again it takes another ten minutes for the movement to reach transports in the rear.

Whenever we came to a crossroad, one of the H.Q. Staff was detailed to fall out until all the columns had passed by, and then to follow on in the rear. I discovered a nice waggon which I determined to ride in as soon as the column had passed and I could catch up with it again. So I rode about half the distance and, since my pack was on the lorry, I enjoyed the trip and was quite fresh at the finish!

We went three or four miles more than we should have on account of somebody's blunder with the map. At every halt the men simply flopped on the ground hitting the earth in any posture so long as they could get the weight off their feet. We came a mile too far at the finish also, and had to march back to St. Fleuris, bedding down at 4 a.m. next to a pigsty. The brigade is scattered up and down the road, taking the best shelter they can under hedges, in trenches, barns, etc.

Our H.Q. are three miles from here, and the Staff have gone up to a field where they are staying. All but me. I wanted to see the town of St. Venant. The country is quite flat and every road is entrenched. St. Venant, too, has miles of trenches, bomb-proof shelters and barbed wire. Labourers are working on shelters for next winter—should the war continue that long.

Have run across a dozen Canadian stragglers, all are trying to find their regiments.

May 16, 1915. Contraine About 4:30, Brigade Staff left for this small village. Sgt Hickey of the 2nd K.E.H. was master of ceremonies and he was some master! He did not know where we were bound for, had only a vague idea of the direction but understood that it was five miles away and promised that a dispatch rider would overtake us and lead us to the right place. After we had gone a mile and a half, a policeman told us that the road was closed. It began to dawn upon us that we were lost in a foreign land and had no money.

Cpl King happened to be carrying a map for one of the officers and he and I figured out the road, as King had heard by a chance conversation that we were to be billeted around here. Our road now took us on the longest sides of a triangle—a detour of seven or eight miles. King and I set a handsome pace. The men were gasping for breath but we gave them no rest and they had to either follow or drop out and remain lost. Soon, the marchers were either on the waggons or hanging on behind. (We reached here about 8).

These roads are the crookedest I ever saw and not very wide, either. It certainly is a great place for to catch an army in retreat, as a broken down waggon would greatly hinder an army in retirement. The roads are a sort of fine cobble; large stones make rotten walking—although all the marching is very hard. Transports moving over these roads make a noise like continuous rifle fire and often we have been pulled up short by the sound of transports on a parallel road.

FRENCH BILLETS

This Contraine is some village. We are billeted in a large farmhouse. In the centre of the enclosure is an immense manure pit. About five yards from the back door is a fountain six feet in diameter which the farmers use for washing and drinking; a brick cistern sloping from the ground at one end to about a 3' depth at the other is for cattle. This is a regular cesspool and our men refused to let the horses (even if they would) drink any of the slime. It is a green oily liquid like thick soup and is infested by black beetles.

The chief pushes of the Staff, including myself, slept last night in the Orderly Room. It was the chateau parlour and may have been imposing once but it needs repairs. Our entrance was through a window and we pulled in several sheafs of straw and passed a comfortable night.

About 6 a.m. word came through to be ready to move off again at 9 and we have been Standing To ever since. The cannonading was heavy this morning but has been quiet all afternoon. Hope I get a good bed tonight.

I sent a Field Service postal [note] home today with a request for a remittance of $5.00 per month to be sent to me registered. I do not know whether the card will go through or not, as there should be no writing on it except signature and date. We only are allowed $6.00 per month and the balance is turned over to us at the close of the war. Six dollars is not enough for me, and the extra $5.00 a month would be very acceptable and enable me to see more of the country.

8 *p.m.* We do not leave tonight after all and have removed our blankets from the transport but left all else on so, if we are called out during the night, we can quickly get away.

May 17th, 1915. Locon, France. 2:10 p.m. Were awakened at 3 a.m. and ordered to march out at 6.

The Dragoons led and were followed by 2nd K.E.H., Strathconas and Bgde H.Q. Staff. I dropped back and followed along at my own pace. When we came to turns in the road (and there were many of these) you could see an endless stream of khaki clad men marching along. As usual the RCDs carried full kit including blankets while the other regiments hired waggons for the bedding. At 7:30 it started to drizzle and about 9 to rain hard. Our greatcoats were in the Staff waggon and we soon were soaked.

We reached Locon about 11. Locon is teeming with soldiers, and columns pass every hour with munitions for the firing line and some big guns near here. About a mile down the main street a battery of large guns can be seen—and heard.

We witnessed three drafts of prisoners go by this morning, about 300 in all. (Four hundred passed through before we got here, while the Seaforth and Black Watch took no prisoners at all—and several hundred fell into their hands.) The majority were big strapping fellows, all young—some sixteen or seventeen. Their boots were big, heavy and new—no doubt good for the trenches but not a good marching shoe. Many wore French Blue overcoats and matching caps with a red band. Several were bandaged up and one poor fellow had his face badly dented where one of our gentlemen had lammed him with the butt-end of a Lee-Enfield. Some were smiling as though glad to be out of it and safe until the war is over. A couple of our men started to hoot when they went by, but they were soon squelched by the rest.

MOVING AGAIN

9:30 p.m. We left Locon about 3:30 p.m. and marched to a farm about two miles away. This place is so filthy that a party was detailed to sprinkle disinfectant. The barns crawl with vermin but it is raining too hard to sleep outside even under a waggon.

We have been issued with respirators to guard against the gas. The respirators are made of squares of absorbent cotton filled with certain chemicals. The pad is about 6" square and is sufficient to cover nose, mouth and eyes.

18 May, 1915. The guns played a merry tune last night and when the 15" gun near here tossed a projectile into the air the ground shook as though it was a small earthquake.

Two graves in the orchard contain the first victims of the Retreat from Mons. The graves are dated Oct.15,1914. Nearby, a large plot contains about a hundred corpses who fell when the fighting was heavy and no time to mark their graves by even a stick.

2:30 p.m. We are now under orders to Stand To and will move off at 4. They think we are going up to the trenches—but I think we are only changing billets.

5:15 p.m. The number of men, horses and waggons continually on the move around here has churned the ground into a sloppy mass. Mud sticks to everyone's boots and the straw on the floors of our stalls in the barn is nicely caked. By "our stalls" I mean our bedrooms; horses are picketed in the orchard near the graves.

8 p.m. The road is crowded as far as you can see with infantry waiting for billets or a place for bivouacs for the night. I hope they get them, as it is raining.

Last night we received a ration of rum. It was a very small tot and had to be well watered as the pure stuff will nearly choke a man and, for a few minutes, he will think he has been gassed. The rum had been issued to Sgt Morand in Gallon Jugs no less than five times, so he has (or rather had) five Gallons for 35 men. The Staff had at various times asked him to issue some, but he was waiting for Capt. Doherty's permission.

This was finally forthcoming last night, so our gallant Sergeant took one of the Sacred Vessels and started for the house to give the officers their tot first, but in the dark the poor man tripped, fell over a rock and prostrated himself in the mud, breaking the demijohn and drenching himself with the contents. The weeping and lamentations that went up was heartrending, and a couple ran over to the place where he fell to see if any pieces of the jar might not possibly contain a few drops of the joyful fluid; but alas! the wreckage had been complete.

May 19, 1915. Raining miserably again today. Ammunition columns and transports still stream by. The chauffeurs of the Mechanical Transports all have fancy names painted on their autos such as "Shrapnel Cottage," "Hay Loft," "Isis," "Pascal's Pride," etc., like canoes on Belle Isle *{island park in the Detroit River}* only these men and machines are more serviceable.

...It has stopped raining and is now a miserable drizzle. We groomed our horses as best we could with only one brush amongst the five of us. There is nothing much to do here, except to stand about and wait for orders.

4 p.m. Firing is distant, very slow and irregular. It was quite heavy during the night but the guns must have been taking up advanced positions. We are now three-and-a-half miles from the reserve trenches and less than that from the guns.

8 p.m. We leave here at 11 p.m. for "Somewhere in France" i.e. about three miles from here, so Gen. Seely said, but that could easily be six or nine miles by road.

It is two weeks since our arrival in France and we expected to be in trenches within 48 or 60 hours. The Police will have to lead our horses, I guess, as we have not yet been issued saddles.

The stream of artillery that passed through Locon today has surpassed anything ever witnessed there before. Would not be surprised if the British were figuring on a big day the 24th of this month, so as to fittingly celebrate Victoria Day!

NEW BILLETS

May 20, 1915. Left our billet last night and are now a few miles nearer the firing line on a farm similar to the others but dirtier. We did not get in until 1:30 a.m. and already the roosters were crowing, artillery booming and rifles firing with noise enough to awaken anyone less dead tired than we were. At the last billet, two men slept in the henhouse and lived high and magnificently on fresh laid eggs. The chicken coop here is too small to admit a good-sized man but I noticed that one of the RCDs had the farm dog tied to a wheel barrow while the soldier slept in the kennel. His feet were projecting out of the small door when I went to wash this morning.

After we left our billet last night and had gone up the road a few hundred yards I went back with a message and was lucky enough to commandeer a horse. I enjoyed the ride, although I was carrying full equipment which is known among the men as "Little Charley." By the time you and "Little Charley" have enjoyed each other's company for a few days you feel like calling him something else! Savvy?

12 a.m. I saw the biggest line of transports here this morning that I have seen yet. They were French and most consisted of only one limber drawn by one to three teams of horses. The horses are pitifully emaciated but the men apparently well fed. The French army are not dangerous looking; they are dirty and unkempt like Mexican rebels. However, their deeds belie their looks.

Since leaving Contraines, water has been scarce as well as bad and one of our Police is detailed to watch the pumps and see that no water is taken except for cooking purposes. The horses drink the putrid water in the ditches alongside the road, and the men also wash there.

5:10 p.m. I rode over near Bethune this afternoon. I would have gone all the way were it not for the infantry marching along. I do not mind trotting past mounted men, but I wouldn't kick dust in the faces of weary, footsore men.

I sold a raincoat, which I bought for five bob, to Mattie for ten francs and made 80¢ on the deal, besides the use of the coat. As you see, my mercantile instinct has become sharpened by vicissitude!

21 May, 1915. We could not move last night as the Bosches were dropping shells on the roads about here. The cannonading is very annoying when you are trying to sleep as is, also, the train which runs on a narrow gauge track between Bethune and Locon and is built on the roadway, like a trolley line. The engines are light but manage to pull long trains of freight cars. They make more noise with their whistling than a Mississippi River Steamboat.

May 21, 1915. Long Cornet The Canadian Division, Lahore Division (Indian Regiments) and all the Guard Regiments have been made into a single army corps to be known as "Alderson's Forces." Since Ypres when gas was used by the Germans for the first time, we have come into our own, and are no longer looked upon as a wild undisciplined mob from the colonies.

Last night, an orchard near here was captured at the point of bayonet by Highlanders from the 2nd Canadian Brigade and this was after the famous Coldstream Guards of England had tried for two days to take it. (And you must not forget that many spoke better French-Canadian than English; some were Russians, Yankees, etc. but all fought as Canadians in spite of the Kilt.

7:15 p.m. "A" Squadron of each of our three regiments have just left. I believe they are taking up reserve trenches, will move to second line to-morrow and, the following night, to the first line. "B" and "C" will follow in succession until the First Mounted Brigade packs the firing line.

Several RCDs have been fined $21 for cutting their long cloaks down into Prince Alberts. This is a most harsh and unjust sentence, as many others have done the same and have not been brought up to the Office for it.

IN THE FIGHTING

About 9 p.m. the heaviest cannonading we have yet heard started along our front. The Germans soon replied and shells were dropping with a terrific crack just below the canal where we had been swimming a few hours before. I think I may safely say we are in the fighting now.

"A" Squadron of the LSH and 2nd KEH failed to reach the firing line as the roads they were obliged to pass over were rained with storms of shell but the RCDs got there and manned the first line trenches. (They had difficulty making room for them as the firing line is already packed.)

It is my belief that a second advance like Neuve Chappelle will be attempted the day after tomorrow. I hope it will be a bigger success. Neuve Chappelle was a failure: the reserve battalions were so far back that they did not reach the scene until the battle was nearly over, while the cavalry advanced so far (as is usual with charging cavalry) that they were cut to pieces by our own artillery.

12:30 a.m. We are very short of feed and I often surreptitiously take the horses out and let them graze. The farmer here charges a penny per pound for oats. When this little fracas is over, we really should come back and make an example of some of these tight-wad and dirty farmers who consider the British as only a trifle better than the Allemaines!

7:10 p.m. The entire regiments of LSH and KEH just went to the trenches. (I find that those A Squadrons were not driven back by shell fire, but sent back because there was no room for them; since then, there have been enough casualties to permit them to go up tonight.)

..."A" Squadron returned without a casualty. They enjoyed the experience and are looking forward to their next turn. They took no souvenirs, although there were hundreds of German helmets, rifles etc. kicking about the trenches.

It rained fiercely early this morning. Thunder and lightning flashes could not be distinguished from the booming and starshell flares of the guns. The Dragoons are still talking of the good time they had—the only setback being the scarcity of drinking water.

7 *p.m.* Just received Willie's {*brother*} letter. I note that American magazines are printing many war stories, no doubt the usual bunk about the handsome hero who saves the beautiful French girl from the merciless Huns. Am I right? Well, the so-called Beautiful Females have two classes of features, figures and manners: *bovine* and *canine,* and the majority come under the first heading. (I will not say there are no good classes, but....)

May 24, 1915. Italy entered the game this morning. We are all pleased, as this should shorten the war by many months.

25 May, 1915. 9 a.m. Last night, Russel and I walked over to Bethune. Just above Long Cornet, we were halted by the entire regiment of RCDs., ordered out on such short notice that half the kits and all the blankets were left behind.

We are to move out at 10 a.m. to the rear of the reserve trenches.

2:30 p.m. Left Long Cornet at 11:15 a.m. Just before we left a shell, fired at an aeroplane by one of our guns, burst high over our heads and the fragments slopped into the drying mud around us. The pieces made a startling whizz past my ear.

The farmhouses we passed were deserted. All had been subjected to severe shellfire and every roof had caved in. Many are used as billets and dressing stations. The side toward the firing line is protected by sandbags and the roof roughly patched against shrapnel, but there is no defense against a Jack Johnson type of shell. You could drop a house into the hole it makes, and the dirt it throws up would bury a platoon—and often does.

We passed dozens of Red Cross Ambulances dashing to and from the Dressing Stations. Some of the slightly wounded sat beside the drivers and their clothing was well splashed with blood.

Several batteries of eighteen-pounders to our left fired over our heads as we passed. The Germans were sending salvos in reply and we could see an occasional fountain of earth fly up.

6:30 p.m. The firing line is 100 yards up the road from us now.

Our present quarters have many points of interest. Shells pour across the sky from British batteries behind us; likewise, from the other direction; fortunately these also go over our heads or drop before they reach here. They sound like anything from a rocket to an express train. Others scream like huge sheets of heavy wrapping paper being torn apart. Machine gun fire is irregular as is also the rifle fire. The howitzer battery concealed near here makes a report when the gun is fired, but somehow I have failed to hear the shell sing afterwards.

Our home is in the rear of some wrecked farmhouses and stables, the waggons under the trees and horses picketed near the hedge, so as to escape aerial observation.

A sentry with a glass is posted in a tree to sight aircraft. When he blows a whistle three times, everyone is supposed to crawl underneath a waggon—not to escape being bombed so much as to hide from the "Observer" who would signal our position to the German guns.

A number of dugouts, some with connecting trenches, are between the orchard and the house, and a big strawstack (with sandbags around it) is burrowed out into the makings of a fairly respectable house. This strawstack and adjoining large dugout, which looks like a potato pit, are occupied by the Divisional Signal Corps. The telephone man is now sitting outside on some sandbags with the receiver attached to his ear while he smokes a pipe and reads the latest London Extra.

7:15 p.m. For the last fifteen minutes, rifle fire has been very rapid. A number of victims from the Dragoons have already been brought up; we will be lucky to have a squadron left. It is worse than when the gas was used at Ypres. There are regular forests of graveyards about here: some single graves, most buried in big shell holes with wooden crosses, unmarked—or "Unknown" printed on them. This must be one of the worst battles in the entire war.

7:30 p.m. The racket is something fierce and getting worse every minute. Shrapnel is flying in all directions. Some dugouts have six or seven men in them when the capacity is only for three.

A platoon has gone to mend the road so that the RNAS's motor battery can get up and engage the enemy at close quarters. This automobile weighs ten tons, and every precaution must be taken so that it will not become stuck and make an immoveable target. The value of this armoured car lies in its ability to move rapidly so that it makes a poor target.

May 26, 1915. We spent a fine night! Cleary, Burch and I decided to sleep under a tree in the field into which the horses have strayed. We took a look at the barn and one look was enough! It was creeping and crawling with vermin and, as we are still finicky about such things, we argued that if the building were hit by a shell, we would be buried in the ruins; so the meadowland for us.

At midnight Sgt Foster and Burch joined us. They had been driven from their dugout by the rats and bugs and apparently were in a delirium, at least Foster was, as he shook like a leaf and his teeth chattered. He could not sleep and was even afraid that the horses close by would break loose, stampede and grind us to pieces under their hoofs. To pacify Foster, I got up and re-tied them. Shells kept whizzing about us and batteries nearby worked like demons.

12:30 a.m. Only one shell has done any damage so far, but it is only a question of time until the aeroplanes hovering overhead correct the range and we are driven out, so we are to move back tonight. It is impossible to go now, on account of the fire being directed on the roads. Some of the bunch are still in the dugouts and will not come out.

I forgot to tell you that Harry Burch, our companion in near-Dreamland last night, was so restless that he finally moved off from the rest of us. He complained that the odour emanating from the ground we slept on was more than he could bear. (He must be without a cold in the head like the rest of us.) On awakening this hot morning, we also discovered a nauseating odour and found that we had been using as a mattress a large and very shallow graveyard, unmarked except by the newly turned earth and disagreeable odour caused by the action of the sun.

Between here and the firing line there is a ruined house used by the Signal Corps as a telephone and telegraph central. Their machines are installed in the cellar, well protected with a dugout and sandbag parapets. There are networks of wires all over, but they are particularly thick right here, many so low that it is impossible to ride a horse underneath them.

There are many poppies in the field behind us. The Dressing Station has a small garden nearby: there is lettuce already and tomatoes will soon be ready to pick. Birds are chirping in the trees—entirely uninterested in the noise of the guns and falling shrapnel.

We get awful drinking water here, the worst yet. I could not touch it at first, but now close my eyes and gulp rapidly. It is treated with alum yet has to be boiled after that.

SHELL SHOCK AND GAS ATTACKS

2 p.m. The firing stopped an hour ago but before they did finish they managed to kill three horses and maim five men in the orchard.

Major Jury went to pieces last night and then retired all by his lonesome to a quieter place to recover himself. I still consider him to be a brave man, who has only got nerves temporarily.

The patch of fire we have been subjected to is a small item, compared to what our boys in the trenches have been going through. There, the suspense of waiting for one concussion after another is acting upon their overstrung nerves like the "water cure" used by Yankee soldiers in the Philippines.

Yesterday, 26 in our Brigade went crazy. I saw one poor fellow taken from the Dressing station. He was unhurt, but was alternately sobbing, loudly crying like a child and laughing fiendishly. Some may recover but death would have been more merciful. Some RCD wounded have been brought through, but I recognized none in the quick glimpses I had, and I certainly did not care to look at them any more than I could help.

The LSH were the chief sufferers from the gas last night. It was used in the darkness, and the men did not perceive it until it was rolling over them. Many were found this morning with one hand inside the pocket of their tunics; they had been overcome while reaching for their respirators. However we have made a successful general advance, and if we suffered from German artillery, it is only a fraction to what our marvellous artillerymen dished out to them. Observers state that after every shell struck, the air was filled with legs, arms and heads of the Bosches.

7 p.m. Another Battalion has just come in from the trenches.

They are considerably fewer in numbers every time they return.

The barns, dugouts and trenches contain great quantities of loose ammunition, bully beef, condensed soups, etc.; bayonets, haversacks, mess tins, even rifles—all left by troops leaving in a rush or by men who will need these articles no more.

7:30 p.m. The 5th Western Cavalry Battalion pulled up a half an hour ago. There are only about 300 of them left, and as tough and rough a bunch as you ever saw outside a jail. On receiving the order to fall in again, they slowly and unsystematically lined up, rifles in any old position and, after much shouting by NCOs, they finally found their way into their platoons.

Their equipments vary from nothing but a rifle & bandolier to others who are overloaded with a water bottle, mess tin and half a web equipment. Most were smoking pipes when they fell in, and are yet! The rifles are of all patterns. A few have bayonets, some wear puttees, but no-one has an overcoat. Every class of cap and hat is represented except dicers and straw hats. Of all the undisciplined crews I ever saw, this rabble has them beaten. But if you think by their appearance that they cannot fight, why just ask the Prussian Guard. These men are fighters!

OUT OF THE DANGER ZONE

May 27, 1915. Long Cornet Back in same old billets. At 9 a.m. quite a number of shells tore up the dirt in front of our field. They dropped in a line, one after another, as though to search us out. One dropped on the side of the road nearest us and—the bombardment ceased. Three or four more shells in that line and they would have had a fine bag of men and horses.

Just after this display, I left our headquarters, without any ammunition or even a rifle, and went for a walk in the general direction of the sound of firing. It was a fine morning. All the fields about were green, and birds sang. It was as peaceful a country scene as you would see any place, and a heavy Ambulance Waggon came rumbling up the road—more like a farm waggon than a bearer of groaning and crippled soldiers.

Half a mile up this road, I came on the advance dressing station. A few men with stretchers stood near the door of the house, which seemed in good shape considering its proximity to the line. Just then the shrapnel started to scream and burst behind us with an awful crack. The stretcher bearers leaped for dugouts and I ran straight ahead not daring to look back as the firing became very rapid and each shell seemed to be falling shorter than the one before.

May 28, 1915. Long Cornet. We left our Headquarters below Richelbourg and arrived about three yesterday. On the way we passed stragglers looking for their regiments, motor cycles, ambulances, motor transports and three large trucks bearing Anti Aircraft guns which look like a Statue of Liberty, seen at a distance: the guns point upwards and are covered loosely with a sheet.

When we left Richelbourg, a Highland brigade arrived and commenced to dig themselves in. They almost make the ground melt before their shovels for, in a few minutes, only the upper parts of their bodies were visible above the ground where a few seconds ago they had been cutting turf. It is a wonder how fast the men become at entrenching but they certainly had good incentives, as German shells were whizzing overhead and searching for troops without cover.

When we finally reached our shed, which we must consider home, I felt my nerves relax. It was only then that I realized how tense a person can get in the Zone of Death, no matter how ready he is to die.

Our casualties have been to date: RCDs: dead: 5; wounded: 30; LSH: 108 (total casualties); 12 missing; KEH: 16 dead; 66 wounded and 50 missing. After a few more times in the trenches, we will need reinforcements from our Second Contingent.

About 6 p.m. I walked into Bethune to buy this book and some soap. There were two or three Canucks there in their motley collection of rags and cast-off clothing, taken in many cases from a corpse.

May 29, 1915. I took the afternoon shift, and spent a peaceful day reading the London Daily Mail and chatting with the Divisional Cyclist Corps men who are always left (when not carrying messages) as bridge guards. Many are the curious facts and fancies told by the men of one unit about the lunatics of another. It is impossible to sift truth from fiction.

Dutras told a tale about the permanent Brigade Headquarters Guard which is made up of young men chosen for their soldier-like appearance. The closest they get to the firing line is not even within shell range, if they can help it. When Bethune was bombarded a short time ago, this fine Guard seized a transport and beat it, leaving the General and Staff to guard themselves. After the battle they returned, just as casual as though they had had leave of absence.

5:40 p.m. I am on the bridge again. I believe that this bridge bears the distinguished appellation of "Pot de Sewelingue." It is officially known as #8, but the board is marked #19. No wonder soldiers go astray.

The boys here call the train the Express Ltd. and, when it goes by, half a dozen line the tracks, while others climb aboard and throw off as much coal as they can. They get a fair haul at times but when the coal gives out, War Biscuits make dandy fuel. I find these a very decent lot. Their food is poor and scarce, yet they try and make me welcome with what little they have.

HORSES AT THE FRONT

May 30, 1915. Gen Alderson yesterday told our Cavalrymen that he was going to recommend that horses be given them *as soon as possible*; also that he *hoped* that they would not have to do *much* more work in the trenches; also that he *hoped* they would not have to go in at all. The General is sure some kidder. (All enthusiasm for the trenches has suddenly left our boys, and anything short of Pond Farm again would be gratefully accepted.)

Coulson, a 2nd KEH on our transport, lost his wife in the hospital in England about a week ago. A letter was sent to Regimental H.Q. asking to have him returned for a few days to wind up his affairs, and make arrangements for the care of his four motherless children. His C.O., Major Hildred, refused to let him go, or even to see the letter. He promised to have a lady call and arrange the sale of his effects, save any little articles which Coulson and his wife had prized and put the children into a home awaiting poor Coulson's return. It is only one incident among thousands, and if Coulson is able to return, even uncrippled, he may never be able to get together another home for his children. It is very hard for a man to get on his feet in England after once going down.

The last couple of nights we have had to guard the horses as they constantly break loose. The web head collars from the re-mount depot broke like paper and the ropes were nearly as bad. Some horses are fastened with rope and hay wire. I saw one this morning with a short piece around his neck and encircling a small tree, so the poor horse could not even move his head.

Neither have we got saddles nor bridles yet. It is very fatiguing to ride barebacked when you are loaded down with web equipment—feels as though someone was sitting on your shoulders. It is impossible to mount from the ground with all this weight as the saddles pull over, unless you have the girths so tight that the horse is uncomfortable. The only brush we have is a crumb brush used for dining tables picked up in a deserted house. The horses drink very little water because it is so bad and are only allowed a limited quantity of feed.

7:45 p.m. Canadians are now known to the Germans as the "White Ghurkas" on account of their lovable, peaceful behaviour and overwhelming desire to take prisoners—Dead.

I had my hair cropped close tonight as the matting of the hair makes dressing a head wound difficult.

May 30th, 1915. The farmhouse, outbuildings and orchard which we occupied near Richelbourg were utterly destroyed the night we left. I have not heard the total casualties, but very few came out unhurt.

About 200 Divisional Cyclists went up to the line last night to bury the dead near there and in some of the old German trenches. This is their second attempt, as last Saturday maxim guns were turned on them.

A new idea in the Tommy's dress is for the men to cut their infantry pants off just above the knees. This makes the trousers just about like what athletes wear at sports. The puttees are wound below the knee giving the effect of a Highlander—in breeches, instead of the usual kilt.

June 1, 1915. About 8 o'clock last night, a great number of Highlanders passed through here on their way to the trenches. They were led by a single piper who played all the time.

The First Division has just returned from the trenches. The First Ontario Battalion had 65 casualties. There will be very few left to tell the story of the First Canadian Contingent at this rate.

Major Osborne of the 24th Gray Horse, one of the best officers I ever knew, went crazy from the effects of gas and fire, and has been returned to England. His is but one case in thousands. I have seen many soldiers here who are properly dippy. Some will tell you "I am not the man I was. My mind is going and I can remember nothing." One Canadian Highlander made the most horrible grimaces when he was talking, while others stand about with their jaws dropped and their mouths wide open. You have to call them several times before they hear you. One of the KEH went grey in the battle about the Festubert line. The shellfire there was the worst in the war so far.

Mr. Asquith paid General Seely a visit today—to get first hand information. He didn't stay more than ten minutes. The general impression is that he could do with a haircut and a new hat.

MOVING UP

June 2 1915. Beaudry. Left our billets last night at 6:15, and came here (a considerable distance by winding roads). Beaudry is closer to the firing line. Our large guns are concealed close to the village, and the French have seventy-fives at work near HQ where I am now.

We are established in the Chateau, a solidly built house three stories high, with a small kitchen and outhouse. Over the front door is a deep niche containing a large stone figure of a saint holding up a cross.

At the end of the garden is a workshop employed in turning out bombs, hand grenades, horses for barbed wire, supports for bombproof shelters and other war materiels. Large quantities of gun cotton, uncompleted bombs, etc., lie about but the stolid workmen smoke and pay no attention to the shells bursting a short distance away.

June 3, 1915. Rifle machine gun fire was distinctly heard last night. I have slept the last two nights in the orchard where the horses are, having erected for myself a small tent made of four antiquated mailbags, and I find my bivouac very comfortable.

We have been given a copy of the Divisional CMP (orders) used. They run something like this:

—*All suspicious looking men in uniform will be stopped and their papers, paybooks, identification discs examined, and if necessary, they will be turned over to the Army Provost Marshall.*

—*Loose dogs running about have been sometimes found to have messages concealed about the collar. They will be examined if found near a camp.*
—*Special attention will be paid to all suspicious looking lights, flares, flags, windmills, etc., whose actions might be used to signal the enemy.*
—*All peddlers and old men and women should be carefully watched. Spies can easily escape detection with this disguise.*
—*All men returning from the trenches singly or in parties of two, three or four must be stopped. If they are not carrying messages, or on another important duty, they must either be taken back at once, or handed over to the APM.*

We were inspected today and instructions read. Any man found drinking water that has not been sterilized goes to the clink. This means you cannot drink water from any pump, pool or lake in France, Belgium or Germany; *I* was responsible for this parade!

I had just walked over to the pump and filled a cup, when Gen Seely came around the corner. He nearly had a catfit. After he had recovered from his first spasms, he asked me if I had never heard orders about unsterilized water. I replied that I never had and that as a general rule I *never* touched water that was not thoroughly boiled, etc. (very glib!). If I had told him that I had drunk enough unsterilized water to refloat the battleship *Maine*, and if I had told him about the filthy slime men in the trenches drink, he would have croaked.

June 4, 1915. Last night we moved nearer to Bethune. Troops pass every hour—and all toward the firing line.

I believe Sgt Foster is going crazy. He acts queerly, and every time a shell passes by, he looks sick. He will never go to the trenches unless driven.

One of the wounded just in says there are too many packing the trenches like sardines, so that every shell is sure to reach someone without shelter and no place to duck.

SHELLING OF BEAUDRY

June 5, 1915. Last night I walked to Beaudry. The shells started dropping just as I arrived. The majority fell in the town square, shattering all the windows and some went through the windows or took a short cut through some of the roofs.

I had gone to see the church, a fine old stone building with a large tower, and of massive construction. Just as I got up the hill to it, I saw a shell burst in the roof; timbers, slates and stonework flew up and then fell inside the yard. Another skimmed the roof and went through the window of a house behind the church; when the shell exploded inside the house, I suddenly remembered that I was due elsewhere!

The road was full of crying women, some very old and infirm. Many were carrying babies, with a couple of children clinging to their mother's dresses. They seemed dazed. A stout priest came panting down the long road, endeavouring to pacify them, but no-one could hear him for the wails and shrieks of the women and children. Pitiful sights like these are worse than the trenches.

The Germans are now massing troops behind the firing line, having brought them from the Russian frontier. They are also amassing ammunition and possibly fresh guns, but she surely has got the Asphyxiating Gas and a new contrivance squirting liquid fire and other magical appliances.

Kitchener may be holding back his smashing blow until the Kaiser has spent his force in the great scene *"Reach Calais or Die"* but it is conceded by all that both sides are planning a round which will end the war before Xmas. All the battles and assaults in history will not compare to the great concerted battle to take place in the near future.

{One book is missing here.}

MOVING TO THE FIRING LINE

June 14–25 1915. New British guns arrived in Bethune yesterday and there has been a continual roar since early this morning. These guns are the things to hearten the boys up.

A Jack Johnson burst near the cookhouse a few minutes ago. It is lucky that a second shell did not drop in nearly the same place, as the men generally run toward a shell hole out of curiosity. The kindly Germans are aware of this and often drop another shell in practically the same place. If their gunner had followed the usual rule, he could have knocked off with the feeling of a man who has done an excellent day's work, as at least a dozen "gapes" gathered to dig for the fuse cap which is considered as much of a trophy as the foxes' brush among members of a Hunt Club.

Le Quesnay, Beaudry. France. 9:30 p.m. Rapid rifle fire, cannon banging, general Hell's Delight going on in front tonight. There is often a display of fireworks to celebrate the Sabbath, but this is the noisiest Vespers I have ever attended.

We had a band concert tonight; one kettledrum and one clarinet, and it was the best that I have heard yet in France. The CSC have a real orchestra armed with instruments captured from the Germans (who stole them from the French) so you might call it an international band.

June 14, 1915. The guns banged pleasantly all night, and have been at it all day with such an effect that the flooring in this loft is rattling itself to pieces and several loose boards fell through. They say that our horses left Maresfield a short time ago and were distributed among other mounted units, so I guess our chances as cavalry are gone for a considerable time yet.

On the Bethune road this morning, I found a number of French children playing at soldiers. They were armed with a broken pickaxe and an English entrenching tool, and had started to dig miniature trenches, narrow but deep and quite good for children.

There are scarcely any men to be seen in these villages. A man in civilians, nine times out of 10, is either incapable of bearing arms or convalescing. A wounded Frenchman is also a rarity: the seriously hurt are kept in the hospital and minor casualties go right back on some light duty such as guarding railways, bridges and so on.

7 p.m. Beaudry. I have just discarded my ammunition boots. The uppers gave out before the soles, but the soles were very thin and I had entirely worn out the inner side of the iron heel. When you see a sample of these shoes (which I am sending home in my crate) you will see what a lot of walking it will take to wear out a pair, and I wore mine to a finish!

June 15, 1915. At noon the 1st Canadian Divisional H.Q. Staff dispossessed us of our billet and we have moved back to the Bomb Factory. I have checked in a further supply of fuses, gun cotton, torpedoes and many cans of a jelly-like explosive. (As there was no-one in charge, I have for the time being assumed control of the dangerous stock.) This "Bomb Bungalow" is freer of rats than our bivouac over the poultry pen, which had hundreds, all as bold as brass.

8:30 p.m. Have just returned from the 2nd line trenches. The armoured train passed slowly up the railway, and Big and Little Willies were hard at it. No-one is allowed on the road in front of these guns when they are being fired as the concussion is enough to knock you down or into the canal.

IN ACTION

June 18, 1915. The night attack on Tuesday was a failure. The 1st Canadian Division took the first two trenches and, emboldened by success, they advanced and took the 3rd line, but the 7th Division on the left were held up by machine gun fire which simply mowed the men down. As the Canucks had advanced too far, reinforcements could not come up in time to prevent some of the Germans from getting in rear, so the result was a retirement to our original lines with terrible loss.

Wednesday night the 1st Batt. suffered heavily, losing all officers but one. George Wilkinson got killed here. Col. Beecher of London lost both legs. He was standing beside the 3rd Battalion Bomb Throwers and some idiot was idly swinging his detonating bomb from side to side when it struck the back of the trench and tore off the Colonel's legs and he died in great agony. He begged the men to shoot him but his mind soon went and he died calling for his mother.

The KEH were in the front line the other night under extremely heavy artillery fire. So, when an Officer came along calling for volunteers to act as bomb-throwers, "Old Charley" scented a job that could not possibly, he thought, be worse than the one he was on. (He was told by a friend that Bomb-throwing was "kind of an artillery job.") This looked good, so "O.C." immediately volunteered and was sent to the rear, to his delight. He was greatly surprised to be handed a bag of bombs and told to go back, get over the parapet and hurl his charges at the enemy's line. Ever since then he has been looking for his false friend!

French postal authorities are not allowed to take anything from a British soldier. Everything must go through the Field P.O. and no

Censor has the time to run through all my writing—even if I wanted him to.

Walked down to Vauxhall Bridge last night, I saw many wounded walking back. Some managed to get a considerable amount of liquor into them later in the evening, and one of the A.M.C. told me it took two or three able-bodied men to get some of them into ambulances. (The men seemed to think these were Patrol Waggons and, at the hospital, they wanted to lick the doctors who attended them.) They had lost two thirds of their number and the survivors drank their fallen comrades' share of the rum issue— which would account for their condition.

No more bombs are being made in France for the British now. The store in this factory is simply what is left over; it is a constant menace as a shell is liable to explode over the roof any minute. It has only been luck that we have not been blown up.

June 19, 1915. Le Prieul. Walked into Beaudry yesterday with Cpl Smith, General Seely's servant. When we got back, we found everybody ready to move off. We came here and established H.Q. in the estaminet "A Mon Idée." The rear line of reserve trenches and dugouts are within a stone's throw of our door.

At 3:30 we were awakened by a terrific bombardment by our guns which were apparently concentrating fire. I certainly would be sorry for anyone (except Germans) who came under those guns. There must have been square mile of ground swept and ploughed into an inferno.

The whole brigade is in the trenches now. The KEH are going in behind the Cuinchy R.R. Station and the others are in the reserve here. Our last draft came today and consists of everyone who had been left at the base, except a few in hospital.

The 2nd KEH were paid to-day. They receive 5 francs ($1.00) per week while on service and, as they had to go in the trenches tonight, they wanted to blow it in case they should not return. I saw Cary, holding a double glass of vin blanc in either hand and one of his friends called out "Double! Cary; two more coming over!" Cary eventually had to be carried out, but he fought a game battle before White Wine finally put him to sleep.

Ginger Clarkson and I have rigged up a dandy little bivouac in the garden behind the estaminet. It is only about 2'6" high to the center pole but we find the ground really luxurious after sleeping on hickory planks. The nights are very cold but we have two blankets each. (Some have none as it is so warm during the day that they have discarded part of the kit without any thought of the cold nights coming on.)

June 20, 1915. Heavy rifle maxim gun fire at intervals during the night; desultory cannonade ever since. The Germans have a captive balloon behind their lines. I have been watching it for quite a while, but every time one of our aircraft makes a threatening move in the direction of the Hun's gas bag the men in charge of the balloon start reeling it in.

11:15 a.m. We have just been undergoing a severe shelling. Two men were killed outright and one man lost his left hand in the transport field where our cookhouse is located.

We see in the Toronto papers about a gallant charge made by the RCDs in which a regiment of Uhlans were utterly routed and their horses captured by the Gallant Dragoons. The despatch was supposed to be direct from France, and is signed by a liar named Hill. Hill has no idea what kind of warfare is being waged. It is a safe bet that he never saw a trench, or he would know that Uhlans (or *any* mounted men) are not safe within a mile of them—if they could get that close.

June 21, 1915. At 6:30 this evening we moved to the end of this road, on the other side of the canal. (The only reason for the move that we know of is that it provides better billets for the officers. The Orderly Room gains nothing, and we are now in a field by a swampy ditch.)

Ginger and I brought our tarpaulin and have constructed a neat bivouac on the banks of this ditch. We were also lucky in managing to "borrow" hospital stretchers; we have a palace compared to the others.

June 22, 1915. This day has been excessively warm, and the canal was crowded with bathers. Tracy and I had a fine dip. The water is quite warm and quite a number gave exhibitions in diving.

There is a story about one of these divers who was down in the water for quite a while and on coming up, declared that he had got tangled in a wire on the canal bottom. Some Divisional engineers on the bank laughed at him and said that wires were *never* laid in the canal; so the diver went down again and brought up to the view of the astonished engineers a telegraph wire. This was followed to the German lines at one end, and the other led to the home of the Station Master in Bethune. Needless to say, the Station Master has since unaccountably disappeared. No doubt, in years to come, his disappearance will be explained by some of the French authorities.

June 23, 1915. 5:30 p.m. Last night we heard French batteries in the distance. The sound is like a kettle boiling and bubbling incessantly. The French have been doing the lion's share of work on this front lately, and they are prodigal in the expenditure of ammunition.

I do not know whether I have mentioned it before or not, but there are many batteries of the French 75's loaned to the Canadian Division as well.

The 2nd KEH sent a working party up to the trenches to-night. These parties are used for fixing up the roads, burial parties or to dig new trenches, fix barbed wire entanglements, etc. The last is the most dangerous as it is done under full view of the enemy's trenches and there is danger from snipers. Sometimes both sides sent their working parties out at the same time and instead of immediately coming to blows, the two enemies worked peaceably, side by side and even lend each other pliers and wire cutters. Such incidents are by no means rare.

Before the RCDs went up last night, Sgt Fletcher of B Squadron obtained some 1898 Champagne and we all drank "Success to the Dragoons" from mess tin covers.

June 24, 1915. I heard this morning that the Mounted Brigade is shortly to return to England to refit as cavalry, and go to Italy. The men will be delighted if this is true, and—why, I always did have a hankering to see Italy or any place where you do not have to sit in dugouts or trenches!

We have been issued with rubber lined respirator covers, also a smoke helmet in a brown duck pouch. The smoke helmet is a closely woven fabric with no openings but has a piece of mica inset for to look through. The covering edge of the helmet falls well down on the shoulders and a party of men wearing this outfit look like the famous Whitecaps *{hooded terrorists}* of the Southern States. A respirator is not necessary with the helmet, but a man can suit himself and carry both if he wishes.

Before going up to the trenches, each unit has what is called a "dipping parade" in which all the respirators are dipped in a fluid which keeps the respirator damp and impervious to gas. A dry respirator is worse than useless.

June 25, 1915. 11 a.m. While on duty last night, I saw several batteries of 75's going by, followed by an enormous ammunition column. The artillery had been not long gone, when another magnificent body of men, the Scots Guard, came by. They were singing "The Boys of the Old Brigade" as they passed, which did not take long: that splendid battalion of over 1100 men has dwindled, in spite of many reinforcements, to more like 400. They were accompanied by two mouth organs and, as they swung by loaded down with kit, you would have said that they were hurrying to a picnic, instead of to the trenches.

26 June, 1915. Bethune Two engineers just up from billets were telling me of a dirty trick which they played on the Germans a few days ago. The enemy's lines first came in for a severe bombardment, and this was followed by the engineers exploding a small mine; the British soldiers then lined the parapet as though to make a charge. Lots of time was given the Bosches to prepare for this charge and, within minutes, the Germans had their front line crammed with soldiers.

The British now pulled off the BIG Surprise, which was the second mine, a real crasher this time, the kind Vesuvius used to make, and along several hundreds of yards of German trenches, over 400 soldiers' rifles, hats, legs, arms, straw mattresses, boxes of ammunition and even umbrellas shot from 6-12 feet up in the air. The engineers said it was one of the funniest sights of the war, and one laughed until the tears stood in his eyes.

MOVING AGAIN

June 27, 1915. We left Bethune about 10 p.m. Every hour was signalled by a halt of ten minutes and it was very welcome as the regiments carried all their kit the entire distance.

While eighteen miles is not very much, it must be remembered that the men carry all their kit and personal belongings, such as rubber sheets, blankets, cloak and changes of clothing, soap, towels, etc., and all the clabber—rifle, equipment, water bottle, mess tin, entrenching tool, a day's rations, 150 or 250 rounds of ammunition, etc., etc.—weighing between 55 and 75 pounds. Then they wear shoes shod with cast iron; train for the event on a diet of bully beef, war biscuits and doped water and finally, run the course on a cobbled track intersected with railroad crossings and mud holes; and if a rainstorm suddenly comes up, we call it a Handicap affair!

I must say a few words about the excessive baggage which Gen. Seely and his Staff Officers carry with them. One fauteuil carries table supplies, cooking utensils, officers' dinner service, wines, champagnes, cigars, fruit and all sorts of delicacies. On the big waggon are their kits and heavy bundles containing mattresses and bed clothing; many coats, changes of personal clothing, saddle bags, swords and walking sticks (both entirely useless) folding bathtubs and boxes of junk which—may come in handy some time. The five officers have twelve body servants and grooms. If it was permissable, they would have automobiles with chauffeurs!

June 28, 1915. We are now back near our first billets, only a mile from Outersteene where we spent the best days since we arrived in France. Ginger and I had as comfortable a bed as we have had in a month, on the thick grass under a hedge. It rained during the night, and has been drizzling most of the morning.

Poor Clarkin almost burst into tears when he awoke this morning. He dreamed last night that he was back in Brandon, dressed in a blue suit and wearing a straw hat. It was all so realistic that he was quite put out when he awoke in France. He has so far escaped without injury except for the loss of six teeth through chewing War Biscuits.

12:45 a.m. London omnibuses have left in the direction of Bailleul and Armentieres. Report has it that we are to do a forced march of twenty miles and, so that the men may march as light as possible, all valises with blankets and rubber sheets were shipped.

I have just come back from a visit to the church and surrounding yard. A few graves are marked with a cross of rough pickets or even a single board bearing the name of a British soldier, most being from the Royal Warwick Regiment, and the soldier's cap is hung on the top of the cross. One large mound has a sign: *Allemagne— Soldats—1914.*

I forgot to say that Sgt Hickey of our transport is now awaiting court martial. He was placed under arrest on the march from Bethune for drunkennness. He had a water bottle full of rum. Others were under the influence, but he was riding and made such a mess of it that his condition could not help but be noticed. He had the horse all excited, and was digging his spurs so deeply that the poor animal was plunging all over the road and almost ran over the cyclists. It is a very serious offence on Active Service.

NEUVE-EGLISE

June 29, 1915. Neuve-Eglise, Belgium. The trenches are about two miles up the road toward Wulverghem. Passing through Outersteene I was recognized by people with whom some of us had been billeted. They called me in to have a cup of coffee but I could not wait.

At Bailleul we turned down the Rue Lille. When we turned off at the Belgian Frontier the Strathconas raised a hearty cheer. I do not know whether it was on the Belgians' account or their own for getting alive out of France.

Since September, the Germans have been within from one to three miles of this town, so Neuve-Eglise is in ruins—some caused by the British when they drove the enemy out but the greater damage by Germans shelling the town almost every day since. It was not until we reached the market square that full realisation of the destruction was brought home to us. The square is built up on three sides with residences and stores, all close to the sidewalk and without a break between buildings save for a few arched drive passages with rooms built over the top.

The fourth side was taken up by the church yard containing a large stone church; the tower is built, not over the main entrance, but over the altar and vestry. Holes show through the roof, and windows are honeycombed with bullets. All the doors are boarded up but, by looking through some bullet holes, I could see that the altar would never be of use again except as firewood. The leaded glass windows were not shattered, but are pierced through and through to the semblance of graters: the holes seem to have been *melted* through.

The church yard is filled with graves now overgrown with deep grass and tumbled and broken grave stones. Shell holes, many feet deep, are partly filled with rain water.

In the square, two Gothic stone pillars, tops now lying on the ground, were once handsome town pumps. One works, but the water is reported to have been poisoned by the retreating Germans. Huge holes, three to twelve feet in diameter, gape in the old street and weeds grow up through the stones. The town is shattered and yet it still comes in for a daily bombardment. Some elderly people still cultivate small gardens. They will not leave the only home they have got, even if they have to live in the cellar. What they live on, no-one knows.

30 June, 1915. Yesterday H.Q. moved another mile up the Wulverghem Road. The Canadians are taking over the sector of the line to the right of this road and the British occupy the left; an Imperial Brigade went in at Givenchy, Cuinchy and La Bassée where the Canadian Division came out. I cannot fathom what all this shifting about means.

The kits which we put on the motor buses when leaving Merriss, got lost. I was fortunate in having my overcoat and Ginger and I borrowed horse blankets. The A.S.C. men had nothing, and their attempts to sleep have been an agony to them. But our kits came this noon: they were captured in the 2nd Brigade, and surrendered to our transport men on sight!

DOMINION DAY 1915

July 1, 1915. Dominion Day 11 a.m. If I were in Windsor to-day instead of Belgium, we would be taking the good ship "Papoose" to Amherstburg from Bois Blanc and arranging for dinner in the Amherst House. After that, cruise up the walks to the Merry-go-round and then an afternoon's Tango and Hesitation in the Pavilion. Return to Windsor to gorge on Pie, Peaches and Toast and a dixie of real Cocoa in a certain house on Sandwich Street about 10 p.m.

Instead, I am sitting in a stable loft in a strange country. As things look at present, we will be lucky to get back for Dominion Day next year, as there appears to be a deadlock on the British and German front with neither party able to advance a yard.

While sitting in the estaminet "Au Commerce" in Merriss just before we left on Monday, nine young men, or rather boys for they were about 18, entered singing and looking very pleased with themselves. They were wearing their best clothes, white collars and ties, tweed caps; just such a crowd of larking boys you see dancing on the platform at Maidstone or River Kenore at a Catholic Picnic, except that these young fellows were wearing in their lapels the French Flag, made of a cheap cheesecloth mounted on a little stick and with the imprint of a rubber stamp across the flag "Class 1915."

Now, who do you think they were and what was the reason for all their bashful boisterousness and good humour? They were the newest class of conscripts, just called to colours, and they will serve for from three to twelve years for the modest sum of a penny per day, unless they are killed before the expiration of their sentences. Two of them were wearing bands of crepe in memory of a father or brother already gone over the long road. They were to be taken to camp for a short course before being hurried to those uncovered graves—the trenches. Can you imagine the feelings of an American youth in a similar case, especially after seeing at first hand some of the particular horrors of this warfare which is not war at all, but a series of long distance murders.

July 2, 1915. Been very warm all day. The Drags and LSH came out to-night and 2nd KLH go into the trenches. They have had a dozen casualties so far; among them, Gordon McKenzie of Toronto who used to sleep in my tent.

A new dugout behind the barn consists of three rooms about 12' x 12' with a doorway and window to each. Four foot of the dugout is underground and four more feet is built of sandbags. The ceiling is a loose frame of two-by-fours covered with corrugated iron with a layer of sandbags. Three wooden steps lead down to each room. Two rooms are for the General's use and one for the Signal Corps.

These Signal corpsmen are always busy laying down lines between the trenches, report centers and various Headquarters, and are called out to repair breaks in the lines mostly at night as many lines are low enough to catch a mounted man. Some are only a few feet off the ground so soldiers, messengers and transport moving at night run into them.

July 4, 1915. I wonder if the watery-hearted and white-livered Yankees have the shamelessness to indulge in the usual celebrations today—or have the Germans' open insults struck home and closed the mouths of the Orators of the Fourth, this one year at least?

SNIPERS

On account of the rolling nature of this section and the many screening avenues of trees, clumps of forest, high-growing crops and other cover, this locality is renowned for snipers. They are as thick and busy as bees about a hive and everyone is complaining of them.

Last night about 8:15 I started out on a little walk. My path was parallel with the main road. But for the firing ahead, it would be as peaceful and more picturesque than Essex, Ontario.

I had been quietly strolling along until I came to the crossroad, when some foreigner turned a machine gun on me, causing me to hurry behind a convenient haystack. Then it struck me that it was that haystack which gave the range to the Germans on their distant hill, and I could not quit its shelter too soon so I got on the path, homeward bound. But the machine gun had acted as a warning to the snipers and, before I had gone many yards, their bullets whizzed by my ears.

Having been merely out for pleasure, as it were, my defensive weapons consisted of a combination knife, fork and spoon and a pipe (which was not yet strong enough to be of use as a gas bomb) so I was obliged to beat a masterful retreat (on my hands and knees) for some considerable distance before I felt at all safe.

Such danger points are common and you can never tell when you are approaching a patch of skyline, ground, or some prominent object that is constantly watched by an invisible enemy. Several Danger Spots are so well known that screens of burlap are erected on parts of a road. Burlap would never stop a bullet but the idea is to cut off the view of certain points from the enemy.

Near our stable there is such a screen beside a road running up a slight hill and from a distance it looks just like a field of ripe corn. We have hung posters near several of these points:

BEAT IT FOR THE GERMANS CAN SEE YOU.

RUN PAST THIS POINT. THIS MEANS YOU.

July 6, 1915. Was quite cool last night and I appreciated my blanket and cloak as I like to undress for bed whenever possible. The Brigade had to turn in their blankets and these will not be returned to them (or the survivors) until October unless a remarkable cold spell sets in. The idea is to harden the men up for the winter campaign. A good idea, this (*on paper*). Now all the covering the men have is their greatcoats and many of them have no greatcoats!

I forgot to mention that just as Mac and I were starting out on our rambles last night, a German bi-plane sailed over. It looked an easy target, but all we could do curse our luck at being unarmed. After a bit, it turned away to the South-West. It may seem strange and foolish to you, to think of young men wandering in enemy country without arms of any kind, and [you are right]. My only excuses are that I have frequently gone unarmed before and come to no harm, and that we get so tired carrying rifles that a walk with them gives no pleasure. However, I will in future carry a rifle at all times unless I get hold of another revolver.

"DAILY HATE"

Today was passing quietly enough and I was having my usual afternoon's rest and reading on my bed in the loft when the "Daily Hate" began expressing itself. This time, we were the victims. About 3:30 the first shell fell 50 yards in front of the house. The next one corrected the range and slammed the roof of the barn. The other siesta enthusiasts leaped to their feet with more animation than I ever thought them capable of, and bounded down the narrow stairs like fleas.

I only stopped long enough to rescue pipe, tobacco and haversack containing diaries and I pride myself on having moved with speed, yet two more shells came hurtling through the roof scattering slates, cement and dust before I could make an exit. When I reached the ground everybody had cleared out of the house, telegraph office and yard into the dugout in rear, except two farm hands who were doing an Arthur Duffy *{perhaps James Duffy, a Hamilton man who won the Boston Marathon in 1914}* across the field toward the house. They took the low fence like greyhounds and finished at the door of the house in a dead heat; it was as pretty a run as I have ever seen at a church picnic.

When I reached our dugout, I found the place crowded and very cheerful. The shells continued to come over every two minutes for the next half hour. Six or seven burst behind us close to the horses, who grazed quietly through it all, and shrapnel dislocated the barn roof and ripped through the thatching of the granary. No damage to life was done, except for one poor chicken. From our shelter, we could see all the shells which dropped in our rear, and we saw a bundle of feathers tossed into the air and found a few afterwards, but no chicken.

8 p.m. In the Dugout. We were shelled again just after 7. Just a few range finders from a different battery this time, as we came in for an oblique fire. Only four shots were sent over but two of them struck the barn and I had one of the narrowest squeaks I ever wish for. Woodwiss lay against the wall when he heard the whizz and, as I was bounding for cover, I fell over him; then the roof slid over our heads, just missing us.

July 7, 1915. One of the Brigades has raised a kick on the everlasting pea soup they get every noon. This Brigade, when in the trenches, get bacon and an allowance of tea and sugar in the morning and cook it themselves. For dinner and supper, they are allowed Bully Beef, War Biscuits, Cheese, a small allowance of Bread and a little tea at night.

They get all they can eat, but there is no variety and I do not know of any food you can tire of as quickly as the everlasting Bully Beef. The War Biscuits have to be broken up into small pieces with the butt of a rifle or a bayonet before half the men can eat them, a number of men already having broken teeth on them.

When they are out of the trenches the meals are varied by a series of stews and mulligans for dinner. The name of each is the only thing different, for the ingredients are the same!

The LSH reports quite a number of cases of sickness, and other units may suffer also. The reasons are laid down to evil-smelling trenches, bad water or food—all assisted by nerves under the constant danger and deadly monotony of the trenches.

THE UNBURIED DEAD

My walk this evening took me across country through farms, all deserted, and over several small hills. The ground is so rich, that shellholes are gradually filling up and in another year or so will be level with the ground about them. Trenches that were quite deep last fall, but have fallen into disuse through an advancement of the line or a new trench system, are now little better than deep ditches, their bottoms covered with long grass and weeds. Soon there will be no trace of them at all. If this continues, it solves what would be a big problem after the war, as the strip of country several miles in width from North to South will be nothing more than one huge uncovered grave with no-one anxious to commence the work of filling in on account of the fever-stricken air which must hover above the uncovered trenches of dead.

Corpses which now lie in front of the trenches (and cannot be reached without too much danger) cause great annoyance to the men in those trenches. Chloride of Lime is thrown out in large quantities; also Chloride of Potash is squirted through hoses, even throughout the trenches. Even so, in excessively hot weather, disease is sure to break out among the men of both sides and, in the weakened condition that many of them will be in, their chances of recuperation will be very small.

It would not be surprising if a heretofore unknown disease would result and not only hundreds but thousands may die before a remedy has been prepared and satisfactorily tested.

Rained slightly to-night and a breeze makes the trees rustle. It sounds like shrapnel passing overhead, making you duck until you remember that it is only the sighing of the wind in the trees.

July 8, 1915. Information has come in that a gas attack is to be launched. Work parties of Germans have been seen driving stakes into their trenches and parapets which will be used for fastening gas machines and hose to point the nozzles from. The present winds are very favourable for this attack.

July 9, 1915. 7:20 p.m. In Brigade orders to-night, men not on duty will help harvest the crops in the district. So our soldiers will do farming for a change—and in this neighbourhood it will be just as exciting as sitting in a trench, waiting for something to turn up.

July 11, 1915. Yesterday morning I borrowed a wheel and rode into Nieppe to the 1st Canadian Div. H.Q. to get notebooks and toothpaste.

Arrived back to find half of our roof blown off and, 6' from my bed, a great hole burst through the brick wall. If I had not been away, I would surely have been lying on my blankets, reading, and most likely would have a few souvenirs.

TRENCH ROUTINE

Reinforcements for the 2nd KEH have arrived from Steerweerck, complete with cavalry equipment—swords, bandoliers, haversacks and spurs. They were wonderfully surprised when they met their muddy, dirty Regiment on foot, instead of dashing about on galloping chargers!

Both sides seem to be more sparing with their ammunition now. Every time we are bombarded, shell fuses or caps are sent to Divisional H.Q. and experts try to figure out what year of manufacture they are and what metals the Germans are now forced to use.

July 13, 1915. The Glorious Twelfth passed off very quietly. A small mine was exploded under the German lines early in the morning, but did little damage. The sapper who set it off told me they shoot off a small one every once in a while so as to mislead the enemy about the big ones that are being prepared for later use. The sappers, all from mining centers in England, speak the weirdest kind of dialect. They are practically a corps of their own as they receive 6/6 ($1.56) per day and do little but burrow in the ground. They are not armed, as the mud would soon clog the working parts of rifles or revolvers. If they should run on German counter miners, they rely on a pickax or shovel for defense. Many an underground battle has taken place that comrades in the trenches would receive Honours for, if duplicated in sight of their Commanders.

The Germans are 500 yards from our front line and you can just make out a head or figure at a distance. Work parties on both sides think very little of stepping out of the trenches at any time of day. The night and early morning are the dangerous periods, for some reason.

Everything is quiet and the men go nearly crazy from the monotony. They say it is as bad as being a keeper in a lighthouse. At dusk and daybreak everyone stands to arms, but the rest of the time passes as slow as a jail sentence. They are cooped in a hole 2' or 3' wide and pass the time writing (letters short and few are the rule); reading (books are scarce and thumbworn from handling); cards (no-one has ambition to play more than a couple of hands); meals are a bore—Bully Beef and Biscuits cast in a foundry being the entree, hors d'oeuvre and dessert—a whole blooming banquet in themselves!

So the men yawn, curse and peep over the trench fronts once in a while, in the hope of being able to work off their grouch by killing a careless Bosche. It would be a relief to be attacked or even shelled.

Four days are spent in the front line; the next four in reserve or supports where the men have fatigue parties to occupy them. Then they are taken out for four days rest.

Our batteries are concealed in woods, dugouts and haystacks. One or two guards only are left. I have seen the gunners cleaning and oiling their big babies and they look like engine drivers or wipers in a roundhouse, after a day's run. Some wore blue overalls and jumpers. The romance once associated with war is gone forever. The guns I speak of are the 6", 9" or better. Only once was I close to a gun when it went off—a large heavy howitzer. The shock nearly threw me off my feet.

I hear that we have hundreds and hundreds of BIG guns which have not yet fired a shot but are awaiting "The Day" (decided on by the Allies, this time). Only a few of Kitchener's Army are over here, and some day we can expect to be reinforced by this army which must number nearly two-and-a-half millions. Whole shiploads of ammunition are being brought over and stored away for a great celebration which will be the beginning of the end for Germany. The Germans are aware of this and are now about to make a final quick attempt to get to Calais.

July 15, 1915. We left our billets on the Castiques Freres Camp at 6 p.m. and marched to La Petit Manque two miles from Nieppe. Our farmyard contains the usual pool of filthy water. A cyclist, looking over the edge this morning, overbalanced, went in over his head and came up expectorating mouthfuls of slime and bad language. So we have it on good authority that the pool is at least 6' deep.

It rained lightly up to 9:30 and then pounded until daybreak. Streams of water poured through our ceiling. The Officers, as usual, live in the house and look after themselves (or have themselves looked after) very carefully.

Before leaving our last billets we received five or six men for the H.Q. Staff. H.Q. Staff seems to increase, no matter how the Brigade dwindles!

July 18, 1915. Yesterday I went to Ploegsteert, a village just behind the line that was the scene of severe fighting last winter, but is fairly quiet now. Many householders have constructed dugouts next to their houses. In the earth on top, grass and flowers have been planted, making a little elevated garden combining utility and beauty; when the town is shelled, they step out and hide under the flower beds.

The flies are something awful here and flypaper is served to the officers by the Quartermaster. The Signal Office is over an immense sewer-pit, and a sluice hole in the floor serves as a perfumery. If it gets worse, we will have to wear smoke helmets. I have taken chances on bad water but here you can smell the water before it leaves the mouth of the pump.

July 19, 1915. We were issued today with shields for our caps to keep the sun off the neck. This is a double fold of Khaki Duck, shaped like a baby's bib and, tied by a string around the cap brim. All the "Mutts" wear them and they are as fashionable as muscles in Piccadilly.

July 21, 1915. Armentieres. 11:20 a.m. The children about the streets all smoke cigarettes, even little boys in short dresses, and instead of marbles or the English boys' tops, they play "Diabolo" with homemade sticks and spools.

SIR ROBERT BORDEN

5 p.m. I arrived back at HQ at 4:15 and found the 8th and 10th in the field waiting for Premier Borden, Gen. Alderson and Prince Arthur of Connaught. We heard a lot of cheering in the distance, as though on completion of a speech. Ten minutes later, a couple of autos pulled up and, while the band played "O Canada," we presented arms.

Then Sir Robert addressed the troops. He said that the proudest boast Canada can make today is in regard to her First Contingent in Europe. He had been told on high authority in England that the 2nd was one of the finest bodies of men they had seen since the cows came home (or words to that effect). He said "...and while you have been busy here, neither have we been idle at home, as we have 75,000 more Canadians under arms or in training in Canada." and you will be "amply supplied with reinforcements when necessary."

An artist might have discovered something dramatic in the

scene, as little parties of weary, dirt-stained soldiers came by from the trenches, and guns boomed. It is lucky that no enemy aeroplanes happened to witness the festivities or Sir Robert would have been treated to fireworks. They have the range of this farm, and would have liked nothing better than to drop a few shells on a collection such as we had here to-day.

July 22, 1915. Met some Canadians who were reviewed by Borden. His speech seems to have been received very coldly. Three halfhearted cheers were given or the troops marched back to their billets in silence. As one man put it "They were tired of hearing the same old bull."

Sam Hughes is now expected to get in the limelight again by visiting "His Boys" at the front, and if he does not get the frostiest reception any general ever got, I miss an easy guess. He is almost hated by the First Contingent.

July 24, 1915. Two hundred and fifty reinforcements arrived Thursday—strapping youths from Western Canada, looking like a Harvesters' Excursion. The poor fellows seemed overjoyed at reaching the scene of festivities at last—but will soon change their minds. They have the hardest row to hoe now that they ever saw.

Two bomb-throwing machines arrived here today. They are a contraption of a spring, levers and crowbars which throw four to eight large bombs at a time, and can be adjusted to hurl the projectile up to about 500 yards—an improved pattern of the ancient catapult.

One battalion has been working a neat little trick of late. But you can only work the game once. A number of whistles were blown in the British trenches, after which the men started cheering. This was too much for the enemy and a lot of heads appeared above the German trenches. Their curiosity was settled with one volley.

July 28, 1915. In Ploegsteert the church is disintegrating underneath the Germans' battering. It is said that the enemy leave prominent spires for a ranging mark until they are about to retire to a position from where the spire would not be visible. Then they destroy the tower, church and everything in the vicinity.

July 29, 1915. Yesterday the 90th Rifles had a game of baseball with one of the other companies. They lost the ball and the whole 10th Battalion could not find it again. So the afternoon finished off with a football match.

I notice one of the Staff has a most peculiar bed: he sleeps in the dog wheel which churns the milk, and his couch is like a crescent moon.

Am surprised and glad to hear that Frank *{brother}* has joined the 21st Regiment. What company is he in? Does he intend to come out in the 4th Contingent? Billy *{brother}* must be about big enough now to enlist and I would advise him to join a different one than that which Frank is in.

GERMAN MORALE

30 July, 1915. The German soldiers have been issued with printed slips to paste in their notebooks. These warned the men against having any letters, books, etc. on their person which, if found by the enemy, would give information. No conversation as to the movements, dispositions, arms, etc. of troops must take place in the presence of civilians or even soldiers whom the speaker could not positively vouch for.

"Everyone, even the man next to you in the trench, must be treated with suspicion and above all, in case of capture, be true to the Fatherland and say nothing. By the terms of the Hague Convention a prisoner of war cannot be forced into giving information about his own forces."

The Germans can still recall the Hague Convention when it suits them to do so.

Thousands of Landwehr (elderly German conscripts) are constructing new lines of trenches and dugouts, repairing roads, etc. These men are dressed in civilians. At a pinch, they would be put in the firing line.

A new weapon is being sold to soldiers in England: a cross between a hand spike and a knuckle duster. It is a sharp spike attached to brass knuckles, so you can either knock your victim out and finish him at leisure or stab him quickly and neatly. The French have been issuing steel breastplates and helmets. Soon we will see blowpipes and stone hatchets!

31 July, 1915. A wounded Frenchman who was a prisoner in Germany says that it was a living Hell. Our officers and men were treated vilely; all were obliged to salute even German sub-lieutenants and were harshly dealt with if they failed to do so. The German soldiers were in very poor spirits and troops on the road seemed to plod along with a look of brooding despair, more resembling driven cattle than soldiers. No longer do they sing as they did in the beginning of the war, but break into half-hearted song only when ordered to by their officers.

BULLETIN FOR THE TROOPS

When misguided fanatics gave an exhibition game of cricket this afternoon, some spectators left in disgust saying that a trench funeral was livelier. To many, nothing is humorous unless it deals with violent death: the more violent the yarn, the greater the joke.

August 2, 1915. Very hot today, the flies are bad.

The Rev. Capt. Wells, formerly Chaplain to the 6th Fort Garrys, gave a sermon urging the men to remember that they will not always be soldiers and to buck themselves up. He said they were a fine lot of men to start with, but he was afraid that at the close of the war the remnants of the First Contingent would be little better than Livery Barn Loafers and Bar Bummers.

Following from a bulletin to be read out to the troops on three successive parades.

> G.644.30 Result of inquiry into use of Liquid Fire by Germans at Hooge Position held by enemy no reply to bombing. Loopholes observed 18" square unconcealed. Sudden appearance of mines without explosion. Then five jets of flame appeared west of crater and fifteen jets east of crater. Flames 10' high on a front of 100 to 150 yards. Germans advanced in irregular groups without masks or respirators getting over parapet almost simultaneously with the fire. Heavy bombardment of our supports followed and jets of flame 30 to 40 yards long directed against our trenches. Morale effect and element of surprise was very great, but the actual damage was slight. No-one seriously burned.

In fact the chief danger, apparently, from this liquid fire is the surprise and panic it might cause among green troops.

GERMAN ORDERS

Some orders taken from German prisoners contain the following:

> War is not a time for Charity and there is no place for mercy in the soldiers' heart. The soldier must be inflexible in mind and body. Soldiers, harden yourselves. In war, goodness consists in destroying the enemy. It is wrong to have mercy on him. The soldier who offers wine to a sick hostage instead of sharing it with his comrade commits a fault because wine gives courage to our fighting men. The soldier who gives his bread to the enemy's children, sins against his Fatherland, for the bread of the Fatherland is sacred. The soldier who gives up his blanket to a woman suffering with cold, instead of taking it to his comrades in the trenches sins against his Fatherland. It is better to let 100 women and children of the enemy die of cold and hunger than let one German soldier suffer.
> The virtues of war are bravery, discipline and comradeship. The ground where charity grows is watered with tears. The battlefield is fertilized with blood. Let toothless Pharisees with distended mouths and flaccid bellies shout about 'Rights of Peoples;' have no fear: victories are your testimony. Soldiers! Be inflexible! (extract from 2nd A.C. Sum. of Info. #256 2/8/15)

Our men are not down-hearted and need no lies to buck them up.

THERE ARE NO STUPENDOUS VICTORIES

August 7, 1915. Saturday. We expect Sam Hughes along shortly to inspect the troops, make "historic speeches" and strike theatrical poses.

It makes me disgusted to see glaring news headlines announcing "Another Stupendous Victory For the Allies." There are no stupendous victories.

August 9, 1915. German sentries always go into the trenches with an umbrella as part of their clabber. When it starts to rain they raise their parasols like a bunch of old women.

Extract from 2nd Army Corps Summary of Information #262, 8th August 1915: *"Two officers (from different sources) went out to reconnoitre the crater opposite Essex Central. They appear to have spent considerable time in chasing each other round and round the shellhole and, cheered on by a stout Saxon, emptied their revolvers at each other without effect. More practice with the revolver is necessary."*

August 12, 1915. An artilleryman tells me that there are 8.45 guns on this sector, waiting for the Germans to attack, no doubt. Digging goes merrily on, and trenches are long and deep. Both sides work continually and even put in cement bases for machine guns, iron posts for supporting barb wire, dugouts innumerable (some with slat floors and wooden doors—all built to last a lifetime).

The 5th Division have taken fourteen machine guns and about 400 Germans were eliminated.... After the British retired from the German trenches, the enemy turned artillery on their own trenches supposing that they were occupied by the English—and there were more German casualties.

August 13, 1915. The Germans put on their parapet a sketch of a flag to let us know that Warsaw had fallen. The designer has his monogram and numbers denoting platoon, corps and division on the bottom. At the top is the Kaiser's initials and the date. The whole thing looks like a Chinese Guard Report! To compound the insult they crawled over at night and hung it on the barbed wire entanglement in front of the Straths' trenches. The following night, the Straths went out and brought it in. By that time it had a few bullet holes in it.

It is amusing to hear the Tommies talk of the "good old days" which means the times when they could buy booze. No places here are allowed to sell spirits. I have heard all sorts of schemes for obtaining it from England, e.g., baking flasks into cakes; sending out bicycles with the inner tube full of juice; Pain Killer; Vanilla extract, methylated spirits....

August 17, 1915. I see that the Teahans are scattering as usual for their summer holidays. How is Southampton this year? As lively as ever? It seems strange to talk about going *away* for a vacation...all we want to do is go home.

Your news of the deaths of the Southampton and Windsor boys is not news to me by any means. I was near Givenchy the night the attack was pulled off and the whole thing was such a nightmare that I could not think of it for days. It is impossible to write a description of anything like that, for me anyhow.

A NEW FRONT

(Undated section. Belgium, en route to new billets.) Our waggons pulled up around the square (like playing Round and Round the Mulberry Bush) and came to a halt among the Signal Section who had left several hours before us and got no farther. They had no idea where to go and the Brigade Major did not know either. We hung around until 11 by which time it was quite cold and were then put on our right road by a cyclists who had been sent back to us.

October, 1915. On the morning of the 4th it was raining hard and the open air sleeping enthusiasts presented a most miserable appearance. The mud was ankle deep, and the ground very heavy, yet Belgian labourers were busy digging fresh lines of trenches and communications. Near the summit the road was sunk and in the sides were numerous dugouts just sufficient for a man to creep into. Barb wire entanglements were everywhere in evidence....

The country behind Dickiebusch is flat, but the firing line is hilly and, as usual, the Germans are on top and we are looking up at them.

Our billets are on a road at right angles with the Ypres road. The huts are poor, leaky, draughty affairs of clapboard. I sleep in the Signal Room, and when Cpl Walsh, Bob Jones and Burnie were ordered up to take over the telephone & telegraph lines in the trenches (and had portable telephones, etc. to carry up besides their kit) I volunteered to give a hand. So I proceeded to harness myself with telephones and rifles and the other three donned staggering packs of equipment, kit and blankets.

Long stretches of Ridgewood Road were nearly ankle deep in mud. Three or four streams on our road are shelled daily and the enemy's balloon bobs up and down like a jack-in-the-box looking for troops.

Battle HQ are in a dismal dugout at the summit of the hill and we were nearly exhausted by the time we arrived. The entrance is so reduced by wear and tear that when you put your weight on the top step you are automatically transferred to the bottom; if you are carrying a rifle across your shoulders, you may be suspended in mid-air. A few yards down the trenches, ankle deep in mud, you come into a clammy subterranean chamber which is Battle HQ.

After a long rest, the guide and I felt equal to the return journey and at Gordon Farm we met the poor tired CMR Signallers. It was dark and they had an awful job to find their way.

There is not much doing on this front at present, both sides being content to hold on and that's all; quite enough too, as these trenches are in awful condition: in one place the mud is well over the knees for a distance of over 150 yards.

October 6, 1915. Yesterday was very misty and clouds of smoke were on the horizon in the direction of the line. I walked into Dickiebusch last night and found the town roads blocked with transports and troops moving in again. It was pouring, yet the men were standing or sitting in groups all down one side of the road, while small detachments were being sent to the trenches. This is very tedious but is the safest plan so that no more than 30 men can get killed or mangled at one time.

Received a prayerbook from M. Breen; with her usual thoughtfulness, she kindly marked the prayer to be said "In time of War, Pestilence, Famine and Earthquake." I was afraid that I would have to read the whole book to find those passages and it was a wonderful relief to find them so quickly.

There are a number of changes now in our unit. The now dismounted Canadian Cavalry Forces will be known as Seely's Canadian Forces.

I gave a package of maps and a book to one of the Lancashire men going home on pass. It was foolish to give it to a stranger, but I was anxious to get rid of it. I will not be easy in my mind until I know it has reached Windsor.

Have been listening to some stories about the spies caught in this area. The worst case was that of a Belgian soldier turned traitor who used to go about at night shooting sentries. When his regiment was in the trenches he would leave them for a while and do some sniping on his own people. He was caught after shooting two transport drivers. Only one was killed. The other brought the renegade in alive.

Another spy (accompanied by a clever dog who carried messages under its collar) worked a large territory, like a commercial traveller, and wore all sorts of uniforms and civilian clothes.

GUNS AND MINES

October 7, 1915. We have been having shrapnel and H.E. *{heavy explosive}* thrown at us all day.

[Continuous shelling] works on your nerves in such a manner that the slightest unusual noise makes you spring up, tense, and watch for the explosion. H.E. and shrapnel, which you can hear coming for some time, have the greatest effect. When the gun that fires the projectile is close by, you can hear three distinct stages: first, when leaving the muzzle; second, the whining of the projectile; third, the explosion on impact or in the air. These shells must come from a great distance as we can see the burst before we hear it. After that the air is filled with hissing.

Some of our big guns send their projectiles over in a very lazy and indifferent manner; the shells just seem to canter along in the air, most unconcernedly sounding *Brrrump, Brrump, Brrrump.* Other shells come with a sizzle.

The Brigade has received 650 reinforcements since we were sent out in May.

October 8, 1915. Walked up to Vierstraat. The road has been fiercely shelled and I never saw so many enormous holes, nearly all fresh. A howitzer battery had moved out the previous night; the Huns had received their information too late!

Down toward our Transport field the Seaforth Highlanders are constructing the *weirdest* looking lot of trenches I ever saw. They ramble around in a sort of Cubist pattern over the fields. Some are not wide enough for men with equipment to go through, and many are a foot deep in water. Yet the digging goes steadily on. If the trenches are not intended as a present for the Germans, they must be digging them for practice, but I do not see how troops who have been out here as long as those fellows need practice.

6 p.m. About 10 minutes ago a tremendous explosion. It was a German mine which had exploded prematurely (possibly by a counter-mine of our sappers) midway between the opposing trenches. The Germans are keeping up a stream of bullets about the crater so as to prevent any of our troops from occupying it.

6:40 p.m. Quiet now—just the regular snicking rifle fire and a little artillery work.

7 p.m. An attack is momentarily expected and our move is delayed until further notice; we are standing to, ready to go up to the firing line. A troop of CMRs arrived to relieve us about 4 p.m. and were much impressed by the noise.

The 4th Brigade, arriving now, look like a flock of sheep loose on the road. If the Germans open up on this collection of lumps, there will be many vacancies in the 4th tomorrow.

9 p.m. Poperinghe, five Km to the Southwest, is on fire.... I have just returned from the lines and tho' the night is starless and no moon is out, I could easily make out my path by the reflection of the fire; it was lucky that I could, as some engineers started constructing some elaborate trenches in the field this morning and progressed so rapidly that the footpath now has a communicating trench dug across it and it is all of 7' deep. (If these engineers are anxious to break a man's neck, they should do it decently with an axe, not go digging pitfalls in a peaceful community!)

Speaking of that reminds me of some of our esteemed enemy's tricks between trenches and near their barb wire entanglements. Pitfalls with a light covering of earth or grass is a very old trick with them.

A better one is the bear trap method. Dozens of huge traps (sufficient in strength to amputate an elephant's leg and having for teeth spikes two or two-and-a-half inches long) have been gathered by our troops. A man caught in such a trap would never scream more than once, for the savages opposite us would loose every available gun on the sufferer until his shrieking stopped and they could sleep again in comparative quietness.

A trifle more sporting method is to distribute bombs and gun cotton canisters with contact detonators attached, so, when a patrol steps or places a hand on it, the charge explodes blowing off his head or limb.

BILLETS IN BAILLEUL

October 9, 1915. In a farmyard between Bailleul and Meteren. I reached Bailleul about 11 a.m. I never saw so many troops in the city before.

McColl, who is still flush with untold wealth, has rented a room near the Chateau. Sam Knight approached him very seriously and inquired if he wanted to hire a batman. The McColl Loose Change Separating Society broke up for want of funds to continue the game. Before they had a chance to ring in the cold deck, Mac had cornered the money market and now they borrow off of him. He is Brigade H.Q. Banker, as he has nearly all the Staff on his books.

After dinner in Bailleul today, I met the 2nd KEH armed with towels on their way to the baths in the Lunatic Asylum on the Rue d'Ypres. I fell in when they again started off, led by the orchestra (one accordion). The asylum, now also a military hospital, has several immense and magnificent buildings. The bathhouse contained tubs in small rooms, but we bathed in the pool in the center, about 24' square and four foot deep. Everybody jumped in, and there was more splashing and bellowing than walruses in a zoo. After our dip, the water was black.

The naked gentlemen lined up for new socks, flannel shirt and pair of drawers. This issue was unexpected so I was doubly fortunate.

Met Robby, who was on Police with me in Maresfield. He was wearing the worst rags I have ever seen on a soldier. His breeches were mended with burlap stolen from sandbags and the rest of his clothes to match. He wears three ribbons, stitched across with twine, the colours barely perceptible. None of the 2nd KEH wear spurs since Festubert, having left them in the trenches there as they were bound to impede a man's speed in the awful crush to get out.

October 12, 1915. 8 p.m. I never mentioned it before, but I am to go to Cadet School in November. I do not know whether it is the Canadian or Imperial Service. I am simply ordered to present myself.

Much obliged to Bill *{brother}* for his tip about the Canadian Censor on mail from England: they are probably trying to catch letters from men at the front which go to England with someone on pass. I believe a package has a good chance of getting through without being opened. If necessary, I will have books expressed, but *make no mention of any information I give you*—or it may come back to me seriously!

FOOTBALL AND FRATERNIZING

These Englishmen are great football enthusiasts, for a blazer, knickers and football shoes are an indispensable item in many packs. As soon as the troops move into new quarters, goal posts are erected—often before the cook's fire is started—and a game is on and I have seen men kicking the ball about while wearing spurs or even with equipment on them!

What was wrong with George *{brother}*? Indigestion, or The Pace That Kills?

October 13, 1915. 9 p.m. A good story comes in of some Saxons who were opposite our lines when the Canucks had a working party out setting up barb wire. The Saxons called across to ask what was going on and, on being informed, came out to fix their own. Shortly after, the Canadians ran out of wire and called across a goodnight to their enemy, telling them why they had quit. The next morning our men were surprised to see that their work had not only been completed by the Saxons but was, by far, the best piece of wire work on our front. Attached to the wire was a polite note saying they had great pleasure in finishing the job and hoped the entanglement would do for both sides.

October 14, 1915. 8 p.m. The gang tonight discovered a place where they sell rum and cognac.... If their appearance is anything to go by, the blind pig has done an excellent evening's business.

October 17, 1915. Last night, Bill Mitchell and I started for Bailleul but Bill's suspenders broke before we had gone far and he did not feel capable of holding his breeches up until we reached town, so we turned in at a farmhouse for coffee. The subsequent arrival of a mob from HQ identified the house as the mysterious "place where you could buy rum." They sold champagne too—it tasted like white vinegar charged with soda but you cannot expect the best at 70¢ a quart.

Tracy and I attended High Mass in St. Waast, Bailleul this morning. A tall man in a uniform of black velvet and gold lace, wearing a three cornered cocked hat, sword in sling and carrying a sort of battle axe, preceded the priest as he passed down the aisle at the beginning. Later he moved the chairs so that the man with the plate would have no trouble in reaching anyone.

MILITARY DENTISTRY

October 19, 1915. I lost the cap off my front tooth some time ago, and have been in several times to see about getting it re-capped. The Dental Officer told me that he did not have the necessary appliances. Neither would he arrange a pass to England. This morning he pasted the old cap back. A plasterer could have done a more creditable job.

His assistants are supposed to have been dental students in Canada, but I believe they worked in a blacksmith's shop.

A broken-down bookcase is used for storing strong pliers, tongs and other professional instruments. One antique barber's chair masquerades as an operating table. Seats for patients and audience are supplied by empty ordnance cases. Victims awaiting their turn at the Lord High Executioner's hands are heartened by watching the fellows who got in first.

I enjoyed watching one of the "dental students" attempt to choke a poor soldier under the pretence of filling the man's mouth with wax and plaster of paris. The man in the chair was spluttering like the last gurgles of an emptying bathtub. Meanwhile, the other deckhand had his prisoner backed up against the wall while he worked on him with a drilling and dynamiting machine run by foot power which made more noise than a washing machine.

The Doctor walked, grinning, from one to the other or beamed out the window at the one-armed and one-legged men parading about the yard.

LEAVING THE BRIGADE

9 p.m. Just been instructed to present myself at GHQ tomorrow to take two weeks Infantry training. The only men to take it are cadets who belonged to Mounted branches and are unaccustomed to Infantry Drill. I very much regret leaving the crowd at HQ, where I have certainly had a better time than I ever expected when I joined the Dragoons. They all tell me they are sorry to see me go; I was known as the Brigade Optimist and they say they will not know what to do with no-one to cheer them up in their moments of depression.

Officers' Training School

BACK TO SCHOOL

October 22, 1915. 8:30 p.m. Cour Solferino, St-Omer, France. These barracks are a mile and a half from the station. I carried my stuff and was all in on my arrival about 6 p.m. The Orderly Sergeant led us up eight flights of stairs to Stores where we were issued with a heavy blanket. Noticing that we were still clinging to our kits, he apologized for making us carry them, as our rooms happened to be on the other side of the square and only two flights up.

This city is the advanced British Base here, and Headquarters for Sir John French, Staff and anything else of importance to the British Army's welfare.

Cour Solferino Barracks, schools for conscripts in peacetime, were turned over to the British at the commencement of the war. They are the usual bleak buildings with stone walls and floors. Washing accommodations date back to prehistoric times. The lighting is a miserable gas fixture, with one burner in each room.

October 23, 1915. For two days we have been doing "square drill" for infantry. It is more than I have done since mobilization, as at Val Cartier I missed (or slid out of) it altogether. To-day we started musketry and are certainly kept at it.

We have to wear belts when leaving barracks; shoes and brass buttons, brilliantly shined. Already I have been pulled up in town for walking with my hands in my pockets. I got called on parade because I had not shaved, but I got by on the old excuse about having neuralgia so bad that cold water in the morning was an affliction I could not stand. Hereafter allowances will be made for me if I turn up with a beard. (I have been forgetting all this regimental stuff up at the front.)

Every day reinforcements arrive from England and motor buses run them off to the station or to various HQs near the line 30 miles away. The funniest and most dismal reinforcements marched off this morning—the poor suckers marched away carrying *lances*. These lancers may be digging trenches before sundown.

October 24, 1915. Last evening we went to the Soldiers' Club where there is a large reading room; checkers and chess, etc. Another club is run in connection with a Gospel factory. I tried to get in to-night to write, but before I could settle comfortably a Gospel shark invited us to pray or else get outside in the rain. I think it is rotten that clubs supported by voluntary contributions should fall into the hands of religious fanatics.

October 25, 1915. Little Soldiers' Club. 6 p.m. Has rained all day and so we have had lectures. Instructors have been talking platoon; shouting platoon and screaming platoon at us all day so that now my head is all a-rattle.

Cpl Johnson, a very decent fellow, allows us to smoke during lectures. The Musketry Instructor, on the other hand, is a demon in disguise: he looks and acts just like Maggie Heffernan *{dour cousin}*.

We call the S.M. "Shiner" not because he insists on our having our boots and brass shined but on account of his first inspection: we were all standing easy, when he screamed at the top of his lungs "Shi-i-i-ner wa-a-hooo!" This was evidently a command of some sort and each man attempted to carry out the order to the best of his ability: some turned right, some left, while others formed fours or marched straight on. It took two corporals to straighten out the mess. We have come to learn that "Shi-i-iner" means "Attention" and "Wa-a-a hoo," "As You Were."

The weather remains cold, but I am having a swell time compared to last year on Salisbury. The only drawback: in the cellar is a large store of wooden crosses.

October 28, 1915. 1 p.m. They are holding a military school under about as strange conditions as ever were, because (1) we know exactly who we are training to fight, (2) we will be fighting in trenches and (3) we are 45 miles away from our enemy—yet we are obliged to study subjects which we shall *never* be called upon to practice, while others, now very important, are not even touched upon....

November 1, 1915. I have met some very nice young fellows here. Every class of Englishman is represented and I believe the best serve in the ranks. Actors, law clerks, and Cockneys who say "Strewth" all sit at the same table now, when two years ago each regarded the other as a leper.

November 2, 1915. We had an interesting lot of conversationalists in our rooms last night. The discussion started with the vision of the Angels at Mons. Both Turner and Cpl Linton, R.E. knew men who stated positively that they had seen them. Linton's informant had eighteen years service in the Royal Irish Rifles. No-one disbelieved him but some put it down to mirages which were seen in excessively hot weather during the battle and subsequent retreat.

He said that he and others had been pursued so closely by the advancing enemy that they were on the point of giving themselves up, when suddenly a "cloud of angels" appeared between them and their pursuers. These angels were not mounted but appeared to float above the ground at the height of a man on horseback. They carried no arms but appeared to be driving the British ahead of them rather than attempting to halt the German advance. There was nothing hazy about the vision, every detail appearing clear and distinct. (A peculiarity was that a great number of the men took it as a matter of course and felt nothing but relief that their retreat was covered. It was only later that the vision struck them as miraculous.)

3 November, 1915. 12:30. Am all packed up and my "turkey" consists of an old mail sack, haversack, helmet, bayonet and rifle. All else I am leaving until I go to England on pass.

4 November, 1915. Blendecques. We left at 4 with about twenty of the Artists Rifles. Before leaving, "Shiner" paraded us, wished us all the best of luck; the Colonel then said a few words, hoping that we would live to follow up the profession of Officers at the close of the war; Cpl. Hamilton shook our hands and assured us that we were credits to him, etc., etc. We were greeted on all sides like men starting for Heaven! Even Mr. Maggie Heffernan looked despondent and heart-broken.

At present there are three Cadet Schools, large chateaux in Blendecques, the only OTC schools in the country for the British. The other two schools are Marlborough and Somerset Houses.

This morning we were given a short talk by the OC, Major Lawrence. (In charge of the 11th is Major Willis, but he had nothing to say, contenting himself with sitting tight and looking like the female defendant in a divorce case.) The Major said that we are expected to crowd into one month information that normally took three years to master, and also some tactics taught by the present war. If we are alive and competent by the end of the war we would be expected to look on Militarism as our profession and carry on the Military Spirit & Esprit de Corps in the British Army and Empire.

His closing words were that we were to keep ourselves "Clean in Body and Spirit and set an example to our men as God-Fearing Officers." Whereupon we were marched to Arcques for a bath, change of underwear and disinfected shirts!

TRAINING ROUTINE

November 5, 1915. Breakfast at 8 a.m. of Tea, Bread and a minute slice of bacon—about enough to feed a delicate canary bird. Still, I have only myself to blame; I am too diffident. I should have gone into the scrimmage with a wolfish face and a pair of grappling hooks like the fodder fighters in our mess. You just ought to see them! A loose chicken in Windsor on Emancipation Day would have a better chance than a chunk of meat thrown down before these promising young officers. Every night, roasts are put on the tables and, like birds of prey, the hordes swoop and despoil it. When the dixies of Tea are brought in, the scramble is almost a riot.

November 6, 1915. Bitterly cold. At 2:35 we were paraded in single rank on the lawn. Gen. Stopford ran his eye down our lines and we were dismissed while he, no doubt, held an Indignation Meeting with the rest of the officers where they would all demand to know What The Country Was Coming To, if these were supposed to be the British Army's Finest....

Fischer and I were mess orderlies to-day. We started in on the simple principle of squaring the cooks. But the Major saw the cooks later and said that Mess Orderlies had to carry on alone.

Nov. 7, 1915. A mess subscription has been collected in the 11th, and we are going to try & better our meals. The other Divisions are doing the same.

Among the work we have been set is notes on lectures; a letter to the Regiment; a letter to an English Bank; a Diary from the time we started here. I will *partially* copy this one for him. No-one here has started yet; in fact, I never heard of anyone (other than myself) who kept a diary out here. We simply have no time...and I'm afraid

I will have to give up smoking and sleeping for lack of time to indulge these luxuries.

Nov. 8, 1915. We had our first parade at 7...to encourage early rising tendencies which might otherwise become dormant! We were inspected closely; after this we were marched and doubled about the parade ground until we were quite glad to be halted....

November 9, 1915. ...I hear that a Reg. Sgt Major at one of the other houses, resigned to-day. He thinks that the course is a farce. We of the 11th have had little time to grouse since Maj. Willis took charge. He has kept us right at work, and it is only by unheard of efforts that I can make a few entries in my diary.

This morning we marched to Hill 77 and had to cover the ground on foot, draw a sketch, place our sentries, patrols, supports, etc. Have nothing to do now except to enlarge a small map to scale; a simple matter requiring about six hours of work. After that, the night is ours—unless we want to study and clean our equipment....

The mess room has four tables with benches on either side. Four men can with the greatest difficulty sit on one bench leading to a great rush at meal times to secure places; another feature is the lack of cups and spoons. A game of Odd Man Out—the Odd Man having no seat and no weapons to attack his rations with. Meals provide all the excitement of battle without the danger!

November 10, 1915. This morning we had work with the Prismatic Compass, Distance Judging and Pacing out of Distance. Afternoon: Extended Order of Platoons Coming Under Artillery Fire; Values of Level Ground and Trees for Concealment and a host of other things and, finally, a lecture on "Etiquette for Young Officers" (hardly a lecture, as Maj. Willis just offered a few remarks and hints on our behaviour every time any point occurred to him).

November 11, 1916. Map making on the road between Herringhen & Rue de Saint. This is a fierce job and cadets wander despondently about with note-books, maps and compasses. It is country that requires an expert to do it properly.

Nov. 12, 1915. I see that Anna Dooley {cousin} spent Thanksgiving with you.... It seems funny to be celebrating during the war, but I suppose you've got the habit. Here, every day is Thanksgiving for those who still are alive and have use of their limbs....

Patsy says something about a celebration having been held in Windsor to celebrate a big victory in the first week of October. We over here never heard of that "famous" victory. I do not suppose that it was the miserable fizzle of the British advance at Armentieres where British casualties amounted to over 8000 (and one Highland regiment lost three quarters of their men in fifteen minutes). Was this the victory you celebrated? Personally I think the game now is to simply tire the Germans out and this winter should do the trick. Next June will be plenty of time to talk of peace.

This course is rather peculiar. So far we have *not* dealt with trench warfare; all lectures and drill have been for open fighting—with hints for mountain warfare! One division is taking lessons in Astronomy so as to find their way at night. It seems that no syllabus at all has been laid down; each instructor is allowed to teach his own hobbies. Military sketching and Outpost (it appears to me) are Major Willis' special fads.

Nearly all the students hope for regiments going to Servia. Brownlie asked for the West Kents, because he hears they have lost so many officers that they are now very careful of their subalterns.

November 13, 1915. 3 p.m. ...This morning there was a drill with picks and shovels: there was as much detail to it as a ceremonial parade with rifles and bayonets but it looked ridiculous. There is also a regulation way of piling them so that there is no noise. Up at the line, working parties are often fired at just because of the attention they attract at night when they start throwing down their spades, picks, etc.,

November 14, 1915. Sunday. The cadets have left for Church of England services.... The British Army only recognizes two other religions, R.C.s and Presbyterians.

The Bath House burned to the ground last night, but the buildings about it failed to catch fire in spite of the united efforts of Blendecques Comic Opera Fire Brigade. All who saw it came back weeping with laughter and said it was funnier than a Keystone film.

The Chief of the Brigade was on the spot shortly after the fire broke out. He surveyed the scene calmly and then ran home and returned wearing a red coat and a highly polished brass helmet. After a further examination of the blazing house, he decided that it was no optical illusion, and the house really was on fire. He then noticed that he was not fully dressed and ran back home to reappear with a patent leather belt.

By super-human efforts the fire engine (a hose attached to a hand pump) was carried up in a basket, and a pail of water was used to prime the pump, which, however refused to work. Two more pails followed the first, but to no purpose. (A little water remaining in the pail was thrown through a window of the doomed building, but the man who did this got a severe choking from the Chief.)

The timbers and parts of the roof which had dropped to the ground were now picked up and shoved back through a window into the midst of the blaze; then the firemen held an argument which lasted until after 9 o'clock; the argument was becoming hot as the ruins of the Bath House grew cool.

November 16, 1915. One point which is of the utmost importance is Personal Appearance, and it is not only mentioned in Orders but, on the first day, Major Willis called the men's attention to the care of fingernails and how they mark a soldier for an Officer and a Gentleman! Now, at Marlborough House, Finger Inspection is a regular Parade and the students have to shove their lunch-hooks out for the Officer to inspect.

November 17, 1915. ...Had a marching order parade with full equipment and filled packs. One heavy blanket, loosely folded, gave my pack a bulgy appearance and was quite light while other poor boobs loaded themselves down with all their worldly effects.

At 10:30 we marched to Wisques on an Advance Flank & Rear Guard scheme. The 12th & 13th Divisions played "enemy" and marched on us from Longueness. We, having carefully selected our positions, surprised and defeated them before dinner.

It threatened rain (or snow) all morning, but we made no start for home and were dismissed to eat our frugal repast of bread and cheese out in the cold. Luckily Volkers had twopence and we were able to sit indoors while coffee was being made.

November 18, 1915. 7:30 p.m. We paraded for physical drill at 7 a.m.... We nearly froze as we could not wear cloaks.

We marched to Somerset and received respirators and smoke helmets, then to Hill 77 where we were treated to a few words on Gasses, Liquid Fire, Gas Shells (British and German) and how to circumvent them. Cpt. Jones told us that the German Fire throwing machine or Flammenwerfer was *only dangerous looking* and that its greatest effect was on the morale of the men, its range being only about 30 yards.

The assistants in the seance then worked a model Flammenwerfer and the old Flammy werfed beautifully, spitting out a stream which may not have been dangerous—but the morale effect on the scenery in front was such that it burst into flames and, altho' the Gorse and furze bushes were damp, they frizzled up. The legerdemain with "Flammy the Werfer" was meant to give us confidence—but unfortunately the majority of the men had seen real attacks where the Flammenwerfer proved more dangerous than Professor Jones admitted!

At 3:30 we returned in the rain and paraded for our pay, but alas! the cupboard was bare when we got there and not one of us received a nickel.

November 19, 1915. This morning couple of platoons of the HAC came up here to drill, with our students acting as officers. (I believe that this bunch we are given to play with are new drafts; as soon as the line battalion calls for help, they will be sent up to join the Suicide Club.)

We have been treated pretty decently by our officers here, but some instructors call their men every evil name I ever heard of! It is a treat to listen to some of these officers bawl out their men.

We are going to the trenches tomorrow for a little experience. It is a sort of practical examination as we have twenty-odd questions to answer on paper when we get back.

TRENCH LESSONS

8:35 p.m. Just returned from shopping to get enough provender to keep body and soul together for the next two days. There was some question as to whether Black & White or Johnnie Walker was the proper enlivener to take up to the trenches. The entire school is busy on similar errands and I do not believe you could buy a bottle of whiskey in town tonight!

My own rations for tomorrow and Sunday are: ham sandwiches, sardines, baked beans, chocolate bars, and one bottle "B&W." (The bottle is to warm the hearts of the officers in charge of the trenches we are assigned to, so that we will not want for information.)

November 21, 1915. In an estaminet in Cambrin. We have just returned from the trenches where we went in two parties: our gang went to the 1st Batt. of South Staffs.

Saturday morning we had a quick breakfast, received a respirator, smoke helmet and 50 rounds of ammunition. Our two divisions had London motor buses. At first there was keen competition for seats on top, but the wind soon discouraged them. It was cold on the bus, but I was very glad to get such a fine view of the country; it is not many who get a view of France from the top of a London Motor Bus.

When we reached HQ, a guide led us up to the South Staffords HQ in Cuinchy Lane. It is supposed to be a very quiet part of the line, and that is why we were sent there. It is policy to safeguard the cadets (at least until the course is finished) but the Germans started to demonstrate in the most embarrassing manner with whizz-bangs while we were on our way, and Campbell got struck in the nose with a fragment. While we stopped for him to dry up his nose, the trench just ahead was blown in.

The Staff Adjutant insisted on giving lectures on how trenches are made up (as though we had never seen one before) when all we wanted was a small plan of the trenches, list of stores, etc. He took us up to a section of a fire trench, and told us to let him know if we wanted anything; then he departed, leaving us sitting on sandbags, with whizz-bangs coming over so close as to be real uncomfortable. We were 45 yards from the Germans and night was coming on.

Finally, we started out to find a dugout in which to hide and we left Campbell guarding our packs. Future and I got a place down in the cook's dugout—a dirty, stinking hole, eighteen feet deep with smoke pouring up its stairway like the chimney of a gas plant.

As soon as we could we went to get Campbell, but met him on the way. He had been hit again, and was starting for—any old place where the shells could not get him. The guns had struck the front of the parapet where he had been sitting and sandbags had been blown in against him with considerable force: he likened it to a punch from Jack Johnson against a man guarded by a feather pillow. We led him to our dugout, and he never moved out of it till we started back today!

The enemy were getting vicious with their guns. As soon as darkness had fallen, their machine guns, snipers and Verey Lights marked time on ours, and both sides just Hated each other for all they were worth.

The Staffords lost one man from sniping this morning. He was struck in the head by an explosive cartridge. He was soon tied up in a blanket, corded in a rubber sheet and the stretcher bearers carried him out.

At 11 a.m. we left the trenches with nearly all the information we were supposed to get. In return for our B&W, the Captain gave us a sketch of their position and the Sgt Major answered all the questions he could. The balance of information (which the South Staffs seemed unable or unwilling to tell us) we six collaborated on and concocted interesting answers.

We loafed about Cambrin in the estaminets until the motor buses picked us up again.

OFFICERS' DRILLS

November 23, 1915. Yesterday we had a drill party in which we acted as Officers; we received many stiff bawl-outs and Major Willis used every insulting expression I have ever heard. It was a good as a show and I could not help grinning, for which he jumped on me and tore me to pieces. He was in a bad humour, and showed no improvement to-day.

His brother was present and we were given to him as a class. We were well pleased with the change as the Major was trying to work us to death. In the afternoon we marched to Westhove for instructions on aeroplanes At the first halt, The Major turned about, spied us and loftily inquired "Who are you, men?" as tho' he had never seen us before. The Student-in-charge gravely informed him, and he told us to send for the Captain to look after us. (He has been very cool to us lately, and I think he has some spite against this Division)

We had an interesting lecture at the Westhove Aviation Centre: a lengthy and detailed talk on each plane. Captain Bettington advised us not to shoot at an enemy plane when it was descending in our lines, as they could do no harm and would likely give themselves up. He said it was a matter of reciprocity, and the British Aviators expected to be similarly dealt with in Germany

Each man had to turn in the names of two regiments and, if there was a vacancy, he would be given the lieutenancy. I was told that there was no chance of a Servian Expeditionary Force Regiment, so I did not give a hang what outfit I went into.

November 25, 1915. We had a 7 a.m. parade today, and she was some Werfer. We were quick marched, double marched, drilled and inspected until Treacher collapsed under the ordeal. He was standing by a fence when he fainted and fell between the wires, where he swung until they pulled him off. 14th Division under Major Willis received equally rough treatment. They were so tired that their tongues were hanging down to their chins.

Sometimes I think that Capt. Willis hardly knows what to do with us. Today we marched, trotted and paced out to a hill overlooking the 7th Division Hospital near Longueness where he made a few offhand remarks on any subject which happened to strike him, while we shivered until our teeth rattled like a Ford model of 1910. After this he called for anyone who knew Semaphore Signalling to step up: MacDonald from the 5th SR then instructed us until it was time to break off.

November 26, 1915. noon. The HAC here are the bunch I met in Bailleul on their way out of Hooge. They have had three drafts since coming here and are up to strength now. The original Territorial Battalion was one of the most select in London, each man being elected with all the formality of an initiation into the Knights of Columbus and the entrance fee was two guineas. I doubt if the whole battalion now could muster two guineas. They are a motley gang. If not for their uniforms, they might be the Punktown Loyal Orange Lodge No. 13.

6:30 p.m. This afternoon Captain Willis called on several men to give short talks on various subjects. I was called upon to tell them of the Canadian Standing Army and Navy. When I had to tell them about our two-ship Navy and Lilliputian Regular Army, the Canadians looked sick.

DOUBLE-DECKER BUSES

The seating on the English motor buses used in France and Belgium is limited to thirteen on top, to prevent the bus from becoming topheavy. Cases are not rare (even in England) of buses toppling over. Over here it is dangerous in still another way. There are so many low wires erected hurriedly across the roads by the Signal Corps that you have to be on the lookout or you run the wires down. If the wire is strong, the men on top are apt to be seriously injured. A short time ago a cadet had his face almost ripped off by a wire while on the way up to the line.

FINAL TRAINING

November 27, 1915. There are a certain number of field glasses for the outgoing class and we drew tonight to see who would be among the five to get a pair...I was one of the lucky numbers.

November 28, 1915. 6 p.m. Had another lecture this afternoon on Sanitation, a very important subject in this war. One new complaint is Trench Foot which was for a long time mistaken for frostbite, but now is placed in its proper category with housemaid's knee, bicyclist's back and the whiskey voice.

November 30, 1915. A. Griffe and I went to another lecture on *Etiquette, War Diaries and Behaviour in a British Officers' Mess or when a Guest on a British Man-o'-War.* It was very entertaining, and many an old fashioned rule was commented upon. We were also treated to a few derivative words in a British soldier's vocabulary....

Our trench reports were handed back to us today for us to see what errors were made. Mine was handed back as being complete but *"more neatness s'il vous plait, and for the love of Mike, leave a margin at the top!"*....

December 1, 1915. We did not get to bed till after 10 last night. The Scotch celebrated because it was St Andrew's Day, and the others just celebrated. About 9, all the men wearing kilts were ordered to present themselves at the Major's house. They thought that someone had reported on the racket; however the officers only wanted them to have another shot of Scotch in honour of the occasion. So they returned in better spirits than ever.

December 2, 1915. Nothing has so impressed me in this war as the sight of Artillery in full marching order on the move. There is jingle and rhythm to an artillery brigade that is lacking in any other fighting unit on the move. The guns, limbers and waggons make a dull rumbling sound and the harness chains on the lead horses jingle as they pass.

They resemble a circus parade except that they move in a close formation so that when the leading horses halt, there is a great pulling up of horses all along the line. The guns are not bunched but are followed by limbers or waggons loaded down with all sorts of truck. One of the waggons had the battery's mascot, a goat, perched up on top. Many of the guns have the muzzles or the recoil tubes covered with what looks like brushed doormats.

Each Regiment is accompanied by cyclists who trail along in the rear pushing their cycles through the mud. Military bicycles are like military boots—built for endurance not speed. Some remind me of an anvil on wheels.

8:15 p.m. Marched out at 5:15; took over some trenches nearly full of water. The idea was to show people who have never seen a trench relief, or a listening post, or a patrol sent out between the trenches just how it was done. I do not think the recruits learned very much. (I instructed Cooper in the art of patrolling, although I have never been out in front of our trenches in my life!)

December 3, 1915. Today the five lucky men in our division who drew field glasses were allowed to select our prizes. I grabbed the biggest pair as my portion, and they now prove to have flaws in one lens. The leather strapping is so rotten that it broke, but I have mended it with a shoelace. Three drew opera glasses, and the fifth has a pair that make an eagle at 100 yards look like a crow a mile away! If there were ever any good glasses in the issue they were taken long ago by the HQ sharks. (These glasses have all been donated for the officers and NCOs at the front.)

...I noticed in letters from both Breens and Galls reference to my books being sent around like books in a library. I would like to know just who all have been permitted to see them, and want to know in your first letter. I hope they will not get worn out before I have a chance to see them again and that you have clipped the pages out of the back before loaning them. REMEMBER THAT NO BOOK OR PART OF ONE IS FOR PUBLICATION IN A NEWSPAPER.

I do not understand what can have become of the three packages of Diaries I sent you, unless they fell into the hands of the Canadian Censor and are either being held up or else have been destroyed. However, either of these is more satisfactory than to have them turned over to a Divisional Provost Marshall and my being Court Martialled! PLEASE DATE YOUR LETTERS. I enjoyed the jar of Peach Jam and the Oatmeal Cookies fine but do not want anything sent unless I ask for it. If I want anything I shall not hesitate to say so. We get American tooth paste out here at American prices, but thank you anyhow.

GAZETTED

December 4, 1915. This is our last day as privates, and no work of any kind is done. The regiments to which we were gazetted were posted on the board last night. I was gazetted to the 11th Battalion Notts & Derbys, known as the Sherwood Foresters as they come from Robin Hood's old haunt, and no doubt contain many descendants of his merry crew. I think it may be just as well to get into an English regiment where a commission is more looked up to and, at the end of the war, I will be paid off in England and can get home as I please.

Some fellows were appointed to Kilted Regiments; their lamentations at the thought of wearing short dresses through the coming severe winter would have wrung tears from the Sphinx.

Our banquet was a great success last night. It was a full five course dinner. The menu was sardines, sliced ham and sausages, Vermouth, soup, omelette, Champagne, roast veal, mashed potatoes and green peas. Dessert was a kind of blanc mange with a thick cream sauce, and Buchanan's Black and White was handed up as the Knockout Punch. The Champagne travelled about freely from the time soup was served until the Black and White made its appearance. By that time, everyone looked quite cheerful.

At 9 a.m. we had a short lecture by Major Willis on our new duties. At 10 he inspected our rooms, gave us another short talk and then shook each of us by the hand and wished us Godspeed.

At Somerset, Maj. Lawrence started off by calling us Gentlemen, and ended up by telling us we were a very undisciplined crew and he was afraid we would have a bad end.

At 3:30 the School Adjutant reproved me very severely for grinning on parade and generally created a disturbance which he would have been afraid to do at any other time, only the sucker knew we had turned in our rifles and ammunition.

Major Willis never even looks at the men of his Division. He has become especially venomous to the Canadians, though I do not think he regards us as any worse than his own countrymen.

Officer with the Sherwood Foresters

SECOND LIEUTENANT, IMPERIAL ARMY

December 4, 1915. After the Adjutant had us lined up, General Stopford, Commander of the GHQ troops slowly walked down our lines. Gen. Stopford had a list of names and the regiments to which we had been gazetted, and he questioned us as to whether it was the regiment we had desired, and if we were satisfied. I believe that the proper and patriotic answer was that we were entirely satisfied but I gave him back that I did not want to winter in France. He looked surprised and disappointed, but merely said "Well, well, well...." Bennet and Bull also put in a holler, and a few others stepped out of the ranks and voiced their anguish, but of course nothing was done.

MacDonald of the Scotch Rifles and I had dinner tonight at the estaminet at the gates and several others joined us and drank the health of their new corps a great many times.

The 13th Division has not stopped celebrating yet, and a cortege has just entered bearing several of them, stiff as boards and wearing the glassy eyes.

December 5, 1915. On our postings yesterday was the name of the Army bankers to whom we will look in future for our prize money. No longer will we parade single file to a paymaster and humbly beg for our fifteen francs. Now we merely sign our name to a cheque and tear the page off the stub—just like that. Some class! My financial backers are Messrs Cox & Co., London.

We officially became Officers at midnight, December 4/5 and to-day we wear Officers' uniforms. (The reason that a certain hour for to transfer from cadet to officer is set, is so that their pay starts on a specified day. and *most important*—there is no loophole between the time a man is discharged from the ranks to the time he becomes an Officer, so, no escape from the Army's clutches.)

A number of men bought uniforms to-day at the Military Tailors in St-Omer and are swanking about with their stars up. The Canadians, or at least such of them as are going to Canadian regiments, are immediately full Lieutenants but the rest are 2nd Lieutenants.

The 13th and 14th Divisions left as soon as we returned and have come back in uniforms just now (and under the influence of the mucilage). They are pounding their natty little canes on the tables, fencing with each other and raising such an uproar that I can hardly think what I am writing about.

Most are going to bed with their clothes on; certainly some are incapable of undressing.

BACK IN LONDON ON LEAVE

December 6, 1915. In a restaurant outside Victoria Station. We left Blendecques at 3:30 a.m. in three motor buses—the baggage on one bus and the new officers on the others. We came into Boulogne on the side of the St. Martin's camp, which is where we marched from just six months ago—starting for the front.

Arrived in Victoria at 6:20 p.m. Got a one horse shay to lug me and my "turkey" up to Bedford Square. Am still wearing my Bucks uniform but the Canadian buttons and serge give me away and the drunken spendthrifts of the Canadian contingents have given us the names of being easy marks.

December 10, 1915. Hotel Metropole, Folkestone, England. I have been as busy and worried as it is possible for me to be and I have had the rottenest kind of luck! Between the dentist (I do not trust English dentists who advertise with false teeth on cushions in store windows), the tailor, the military outfitters and the box makers, I have had a dog's life.

My clothes were delivered last night and this morning I came out in my new glad rags. Buying a trousseau for a bride is not 1,2,3 with equipping a new officer and I had to undertake the journey alone and go the limit from cap to shoes—even the dinky walking stick!

At Canadian Pay Department, I wheedled 30 pounds out of the house; it was not all that is coming to me, but I could get no more. The number employed there is very large and I was surprised to see so many able-bodied men who came out to take a poke at the Kaiser now delighted to escape the horrors of war. A large number of Canucks came rolling up in taxicabs to draw what they could; some walked and some could not walk, but were assisted by friends....

I have an extra day's leave granted for the purpose of coming to Shorncliffe to obtain my discharge from the Canadian Army, and I am expected at St-Omer on Saturday. Boats run whenever the Captain feels like starting.

I was to report to the Commander of the Cdn Forces Depot, Shorncliffe. He listened to my tale of woe, and told me to see the ABC or XYZ (or something) at 21 Earls Road in Folkestone. I told him that I would like a few days to finish off my business and he said "Certainly. How long do you want? How about the 20th of December? Will that do?" I managed to keep a straight face and tell him that that would do nicely.

When I got to Folkestone, the "alphabet" at Earls Road was out to lunch. At 2:30 I was again on the job but the mysterious gentleman had gone to London, so I was referred to the Adjutant; to Major Kirkly; then to Capt. Carey; and then to Sgt Baker in the Canadian Cavalry Office, Somerset Barracks—back in Shorncliffe.

This time, I got a taxicab. At the Orderly room I waited while an orderly ran out to find Sgt Baker. He arrived, drunk and perfectly incapable; however he started to write out sheet after sheet of Army forms; Doctor's certificates; pay applications; discharge applications; conduct sheets; etc. About 4:30 he announced that all that was necessary was the Colonel's signature but, as the Colonel was out, I would have to come back the following morning. I could have shot him with pleasure.

I returned to Folkestone and here I am in Room 233 of the Metropole Hotel—tired out and mad enough to smash an egg!

December 11, 1915. Set off once more for Shorncliffe. Sgt Baker, who was sobering up, *positively* assured me that my papers had been sent down to 21 Earls Road and I was about to leave when I caught sight of them on the desk. He apologized, and assured me that he had mistaken me for someone else. Another half hour, and then I was received by Col. (signature indecipherable, but it looks like Bat Masterson). He signed and wished me the "best of luck" (a horrible expression always used in this war by people who think that something is going to "done happen to that man").

After receiving the discharge papers, I returned to Earls Road and Capt. Carey presented me with a railway warrant. I got another warrant (First Class) to London from the Embarkation Officers at Folkestone. (I could have got more if I had tried. All that was necessary was to tell a little tale and draw your ticket or warrant for same.) I now have a few days to loaf around.

Many Canadians wander about Folkestone and Shorncliffe: most have never been out of England and, of course, draw more money and put on more swank than the fighting men. The biggest loafers and worst bums in the lot I saw were our old friends the 6th Fort Garry Horse. Freddy H— who was in "C" 4th Troop is now an OR Sergeant. (He told me in Maresfield that he would desert sooner than go to France and he wanted me to desert with him.) Some of his Staff brothers look to be the same stamp as himself. Yet when this crowd go back, they will possibly get more honours than men who have been through the mill.

RECRUITING

Recruiting goes merrily on. Every time I pass Trafalgar Square an immense crowd is gathered on one side of the Nelson column while Recruiting Sergeants harangue the men from the steps and soldiers pass through the crowd urging men to Come Up to the Colours. Every once in a while some civilian who can no longer stand the pressure mounts the steps and accepts the King's shilling. It reminds me of nothing so much as a Salvation Army revival where people are pleaded with to come up and be saved while the band plays and exhorters wearing different stripes and shoulder badges give testimony as to the advantages and luxurious living to be had in the Army. *"Join now, boys, and spend a delightful winter in the trenches! All the comforts of home and 26 cents a day pocket money— perhaps!"*

London. Charing Cross. 2:30 p.m. Dinner in Lyons Corner House. Some place this. Full orchestra, many officers, private soldiers, corporals and women. A balcony upstairs, running around the room. It is one of the "night restaurants" spoken of in the *Times* as being the scenes of disgraceful revelry on the part of officers and men wearing His Majesty's uniform.

December 14, 1915. With Dr. and Mrs Neville, South Ascot, Berkshire. On leave. I went to Cox and Co. and they furnished me with a cheque book; as soon as I join the new regiment, my pay (about ten shillings per day) will be put to my credit.

We are expected to live up to our pay: the British Army wants its officers to live like Officers, and not eat their meals at Beefsteak

Tony's, or board at Sloppy Eliza's! All transportation must be first class on railways.

I went to confession Saturday night and Sunday went to the early Mass. It is about a year since I was last at communion, in the same St. Patricks church.

I took a walk to Trafalgar Square and saw the famous Girls' Church League Band: they were out to assist the Finsbury Rifles Recruiting Drive. Their uniforms were very natty, blue with yellow trimming and a red cockade in a colonial hat; their instruments, drums, etc. were slung by red sashes. They rather looked like a burlesque chorus.

The centre of the platform was occupied by a tall man in frock coat and silk hat. This gentleman ramped, roared and raved up and down, shaking his fist at the crowd and stamping his feet.

On the opposite side, a rival Recruiting Society was at work, and their lineup consisted of a row of young fellows in red coats who filled in the back of the scene like the preliminary outdoor exhibition of a sideshow. Their barker seemed to be pointing at the men and explaining the merits of each individual. Meanwhile, soldiers with recruiting ribbons in their caps, went through the crowd interviewing desirables while women with baskets distributed White Feathers. I was sorry that I couldn't obtain a feather, as my pipe needed cleaning, but I was in uniform and therefore exempt.

December 14, 1915. Ravensdale House. See a lot of independent looking niggers wearing W.I.R. Badges on their shoulders. I believe they are part of a contingent from the West Indies.

RETURN TO FRANCE

December 20, 1915. Hotel Louvre, Boulogne. Left Victoria Station at 9:50 a.m. on the usual long slow train. Embarked without loss of time, and had a fair passage, although it is said that the returning transport hit floating mines.

December 21, 1915. en route to the front. 2 p.m. "On a troop train through Northern France" would be a good name for a dirge as we travel at a walking pace over a most melancholy road. When we left Victoria on Monday, some piper was on the job, and had his bagpipe wailing the most awful banshees. I had hoped to be rid of this fellow when he played us off the steamer at the quai yesterday, but he is aboard this train and at each station he tunes up his horrible pipes.

I rose at 7:30 and had an omelette and coffee strong enough to vote. We left Boulogne at 1:10. The country is flooded as a result of late heavy rains.

6:20 p.m. Very dark outside and chilly in these carriages. I have just discovered that Steenbecque is where I should have got out after all! I will have to go back from the next station. It seems that a great many of the 8th division are hopelessly lost.

December 22, 1915. Steenbecque Village. Last night, myself and eight others were landed at some station up the line. At 7 p.m. the RTO put us on a coal train leaving for Steenbecque where he thought my Division was located. (I thought that the 11th Notts were in the 25th Brigade, because it said so on my pass.) That coal train was the slowest thing I have seen yet, and we did not land at Steenbecque till nearly 7:40 p.m. The RTO here told me that the 25th Brigade was at Cercius and the best thing I could do was to walk to HQ at Mauberck and get a transport for Cercius. I walked up to Mauberck but they are on manoeuvres, so there was nothing to do but return to the RTOs office.

A corporal gave me space in the post office (a disused box car) and I made a bed in my valise. At 7:45 this morning, I caught a lorry for the 25th brigade but before going very far, I was told that the 11th Notts were now in the 70th brigade! So I was dished again at the mail dump. The 11th Notts waggon shortly pulled up, and the corporal made his bow before me, and I was on the right road at last.

WITH THE SHERWOOD FORESTERS

Arrived here, I found the Battalion away, with only a few men left under 2nd Lieutenant Hayes. He is a very nice fellow. I am billeting with him, and his man Dale is looking after us until the Battalion returns.

December 23, 1915. Didn't get up till 7:45 when Hayes' man called us and it was twenty minutes before Hayes saw fit to show a leg. He says that they have an easy time of it here; they get fed up with having nothing to do but sleep. This job could suit me fine!

The 11th Notts & Derbys are the last Service Battalion raised, and the 12th are still in England, only sending out drafts when required. Kitchener's Krush have been in training for over a year and, though they came to France in August, are *still* training.

What surprises me is how they came to be put in the 8th Division which is made up of regulars and well-trained Territorials. Hayes said it was a compliment on their efficiency. That may be so; or they may be so rotten that they put them with a first class division in hopes of bracing them up and making something of them in time!

I walked through the camp this morning. There is mud ankle deep all over but the bell tents are well drained, and brick walks and trench boards are laid in regular paths. Neatness and cleanliness predominate everywhere, and there should be no cause for the awful conditions to which we were subjected at Pond Farm last winter.

English officers certainly look after their own comfort, and their men take a more servile attitude toward them than anything I ever saw before except a Southern nigger. (The free and easy Canadians would not make a hit here.)

This battalion is going to do very well at Christmas. The Orderly Officer's room is lined with boxes shoulder high containing presents from the Daily Sketch's Contribution Fund, The Overseas Club, the Queen's Gifts, a couple of waggons of boxes from the City of Nottingham and the counties of Notts and Derby!

2 *p.m.* The battalion has just marched in. They look like husky fellows, and should be able to do their bit. This battalion has only been in the trenches a few times. I do not think they have never been subjected to severe shelling, and have no idea what a battle or charge looks like.

December 24, 1915. "A" Company's hut. After the battalion returned yesterday, I presented myself to Lt Col. Watson. He said he had been instructed that I was to be sent on leave as soon as I had reported. I said that the Canadian Army had granted me ten days in England.

These officers get leave every three months—five days in England. When they heard that I had just had my first leave in eight months, they were thunderstruck.

I was introduced to Captain J.E. Carr, O.C. of A Company, and he made me at home at once. I am appointed to No. 4 Platoon and was invited to take the inspection. My sergeants are A1 and the Platoon Sergeant carries three ribbons: Kings and Queens, South African and Indian Frontier.

CHRISTMAS 1915

December 25, 1915. Christmas Day. Nothing much to do yesterday and nothing at all today. Company A and B officers mess together and they are as fine a bunch of fellows as I have met out here yet. A few are more or less sane, but the majority are crazy and it sounds like our dining room in Windsor at mealtimes, only the language and stories retailed here are generally not so high class!

In A Company we have Captain Cam, Lt Martin (who is absolutely bughouse but one of the nicest fellows I have met), 2nd Lieut. Willie Green, Fred Archer and myself. In our hut, we also have Lieut. Gaskell, affectionately known as "Pa."

B Company staff are Captain Brennan, Lieut. Maitland, (Bombing Officer); Humphreys (Signalling); 2nd Lieutenants Bosworth, Woodcock and Manistee. The whole bunch stick together like a family.

Our daily routine is as follows: Reveille at 7, but I am the only one who gets up; the rest lounging out half an hour later. I am handed tea and my servant, Ainsworth, has my clothes brushed, shoes buffed, and everything laid out for me to put on; he helps me into my tunic, gives my cap a few final brushes, and bows himself out.

The first parade at 9 a.m. keeps us busy till lunch, and we may attend drills or lectures from 2 until 4 p.m. Every afternoon, mail is put out to be censored. One letter out of every ten or fifteen is read.

Breakfast consists of oatmeal; ham or bacon and an egg and sausage or herring, tea, toast and butter, or bread and butter and jam.

Lunch—a slice of joint, or minced meat or a steak, potatoes and one other vegetable. For desert, rice pudding, prunes or canned peaches; whiskey and Perrier Water.

For tea we have bread and butter, cake and sometimes cold meat. Then we loaf about until dinner, lasting anywhere from an hour and a half to three hours depending upon the amount of drink consumed.

For dinner at 7—soup, fish; beef or lamb; potatoes and vegetable, dessert; whiskey and Perrier, port, coffee, fruit, candy & figs or dates, etc. We do very well, as you can see.

Before we go to bed another stiff jolt of booze is laid in the stomach.

December 26, 1915. I am the only R.C. Officer in the battalion and I took the parade from here to Steenbecque church yesterday. The priest while calling the roll, praised my men [for their good attendance]. It amused me when he asked the Yorks and Lancasters to stand up and he bawled out the corporal in charge; then he inspected another Battalion's selection—and bawled them out too.

We had a great blowout last night, without doubt the best spread in the Battalion: certainly no-one else had a turkey as our Mess President bought the last one in the British Canteen and it was only got by judicious bribery as it had been previously sold three times.

After dinner the subs from other companies wandered in and of course we drank their health, and they drank ours and another to absent friends, and to the King etc., etc. I broke away with difficulty before they got properly started.

I have been received by the mess as a brother, and could not possibly have fallen in with a better set of fellows. I must say that I am enjoying the time of my life.

It is rumoured that we go into the trenches again on January 3rd or 4th.

WAITING FOR ORDERS

December 29, 1915. We have had no rain today, but this is exceptional. If it does not rain during the day, it pours all night. The parades are a nightmare, as mud is ankle deep or more on the parade grounds, and the men are obliged to move very slowly.

I received today: two bundles of Catholic Records, a letter from Marg Breen and a box from a Miss H. Murphy, in London. (The box contained holy cards, so the Breens are at the bottom of it.) It also contained Black Cat cigarettes, soup cubes, black sticky candy (the kind three year old kids usually have sticking to their fingers and mouths) and badly decomposed bananas.

The eternal saluting gets on my nerves. You can hardly step outside but what you are saluted a dozen times and working parties stand like ramrods, frozen faced, until you pass by.

An officer commands more respect among the English regiments than among the Colonial—and he had better live up to the standards or they soon run him down. Some of the men have very hard characters, according to their form sheets (I mean conduct sheets) but the sergeants are the men who have trouble with them.

The majority of Sherwood Foresters are miners. From censoring their letters, I have formed a very good opinion of them, and find them writing the most cheerful letters, congratulating themselves on being out of the trenches for the holidays, and telling their friends and relatives to "keep smileing!" When you read these, you begin to realize just what some of them have given up to serve their country. Quite a number are addressed to brothers in other battalions, and often I see some reference to "our Joe" who has not been heard of since the last attack.

January 1, 1916. Sherwood Foresters Officers' Mess. We had a wild time last night. The band played, and we had an impromptu concert during the intervals. A waiter stationed near each table saw that no-one wanted for Champagne, port or whiskey, cigarettes or stogies. At 11:55 Col. Watson proposed a toast to 1916, the band struck up Auld Lang Syne and we ushered 1915 out in state.

January 2, 1916. In French towns, the squares are infested with children who prey on officers. Martin and I were attacked last night. One little fellow, about 7, was so pressing in his demands for *baksheesh* that Martin started to run down the street and the kid pelted along behind him, much to the amusement of some Tommies standing around.

January 3, 1916. I got three volunteers for wire-cutting work. No-one in the 16th volunteered. Wirecutters are not considered good risks. The men get a fit of shyness when volunteers are called, but I am going to see that one or two in each section will be competent to do the work when called upon.

January 4, 1916. We had a nine-mile route march this morning. Every time we passed through a hamlet, the band played and the villagers turned out to see us go by. I'm sorry to say we had one man of A company fall out on the road. I went to see what was wrong and he looked exhausted, so I carried his rifle for him.

It rains every night and the grounds are ankle deep in mud. On parade, the men shift about trying to find a place to stand with a minimum of discomfort.

January 5, 1916. After lunch we have orderly room reports, crime sheets to enter, letters to censor and Orders for next day to read. I keep busy, but the other officers indulge in auction bridge which is all the rage. They play for a franc a rubber and some lose the best part of their pay at this seductive game.

January 7, 1916. Thursday morning, this Battalion marched to Molinghem—a formal visit to a brigade of Foresters billeted there. Our soccer-football team had arranged to play a match.

We reached Isbert about 11:15 and from there to our camping grounds men from the 8th Battalion kept flocking out to the road and calling to their friends and relatives in our ranks. It was like a family reunion when the battalions got together and brothers, cousins, even fathers and sons were united for a time.

The game started at 2, and all the goals were scored in the first half of play, which was very good but in no way as exciting as the second half. The rooting was enthusiastic, but to a baseball fan it would sound weak and consumptive.

After tea, one of officers said that we were to march off at 4:30, so we loafed about till 4:35 and then started for the grounds. Imagine our horror when we found the procession hiking along the road led by the Colonel, with the Battalion Band and not an officer in sight. All the other officers, including ourselves, joined the parade in the road.

This 8th Battalion Sherwood Foresters' Band is famous among our First Contingent, as it played our exhausted soldiers out of Ypres after the gas attack. Last night it played out of Molinghem the last troops (other than its own) which it will play out of France; today the Foresters Brigade and the rest of the 46th leave for Marseilles, and thence for Egypt and East Africa.

The last I saw of them was the band standing in front of the Isbeques church playing the famous March Past of the Sherwood Foresters, "The 95th" or "I am 95 Today." They are quite perked up about leaving for Africa and the rumour that the Germans have submarines in the Mediterranean causes no worry.

ON THE MOVE

January 8, 1916. We are moving on Monday to the line below Armentières, so this morning the doctor had medical inspection. For this the men had to stand well nigh naked and wait for the doctor to come along. It is no joke and I was very sorry for the poor shivering fellows.

January 9, 1916. 11.30 a.m. At present the band is on a platform erected next to the mess. Several dozen men are gathered about them and more, in front of their tents. These men are great lovers of music, and all take pride in our band.

Sgt Shaw has met several old soldiers in this country who have billeted themselves at some farmhouse ever since the retreat from Mons, living off the fat of the land and dodging the British Army. They do a little work on the farms in return for their keep. Of course they are old regulars who know all the ropes and after the war, they will return to England with some yarn about having lost their memory or having been kept prisoner in Germany.

January 10, 1916. Neuf-Berquin. Left camp at 8:30 a.m. All the men were heavily laden, and marched with their usual slow pace. Territorials cannot march as fast as the Canadians.

A number of men in our companies fell out and two of from No. 4 wished to do so. I would not let them, and kidded them to continue on. As a result, mine was the only platoon to finish tonight without losing a man. The Yorks and Lancs kept losing a man here and there along the road, like paper in a paper chase.

There are several reasons for men giving up on a march besides fatigue or weakness. First, they do not properly pack their equipment: instead of making the kit compact, they hang mess tins, mugs, kettles, etc., all over them, until they look like Christmas trees. It's nothing rare to see a man with his bayonet or entrenching tool hanging so loose that it bangs against his legs at every step— and he looks insulted when I make him do it up.

Secondly, some platoons march badly because they do not step all together: they sound more like a flock of sheep than a body of troops, and they tire quickly. This also causes "march hypnotism:" men look at the feet of the man in front or, perhaps, a swinging mess tin on the back of their lead man; they go for some distance with their eyes focussed on the object until, suddenly, they emit a few shrieks and fall down on the road.

The third reason for men falling out, is that they want esprit de corps: they lack pride in their sections. I am proud that our platoon lasted so well, although the march was only over about fifteen miles of road, all in rotten condition except for five or six miles of cobbles. I cannot make up my mind whether I prefer the cobbles or ankle deep mud! Both can become such a bore.

I was very sorry for our chaps: many were staggering under their loads. At every 10 minute halt, they lay down with the loads still on their backs, or took off the pack, and collapsed on top of it. I never before noticed the number of old men in the battalions but, as some lay by the road today completely done up, every year of their life showed up.

Arrived here at 4:30. A Company is billeted in a large barn and the men seem quite comfortable.

January 11, 1916. Left our billet this morning at 9, formed up outside of Neuf-Berquin and marched to Estairs. The band played us on until we came in sight of Sailly when (on account of our nearness to the German lines) the band ceased its good work. From this point on, the Battalion advanced in companies at 10 minute intervals. When we reached the wide road which runs to the trenches, the companies advanced by platoons at five-minute intervals so that only one platoon would suffer from any demonstration on the road.

We relieved the 12th Battalion of the Rifle Brigade and are now occupying the advanced support billet about 1000 yards from our front line and 1060 yards from the enemy's line. This is called "Windy Post" and is supposed to be subject to severe shell fire but it looks all right. A battery of RFA just behind the barn fire over our roof.

THE RUTLAND ARMS

No. 1 Platoon of A Company occupy part of a double house, together with all our officers and 2nd Lts Kemball and Rogers of C who had their billets knocked to pieces this morning. The whole shebang passes under the imposing name of "The Rutland Arms" and a notice board over the main entrance—a battered door with a string latch—announces the fact to unsuspecting visitors.

We are quite comfortable as our valises came up on the transport and are now laid out on little piles of straw. Nothing could be warmer than a valise or sleeping bag with blankets and a trench coat on top. Illumination is the customary candle in the bottle and the broken windows are boarded at night, screened with a curtain made of empty sandbags.

Another large room contains a battered-in fireplace; a good oak table; a rough bench; cane-bottomed chairs and a picture of the Crucifixion over the mantel. There is nothing we could add unless perhaps a crocheted motto like "God Bless Our Home."

Everyone seems much afraid of the gas and all ranks carry smoke or tube helmets at all times, even wearing them at night. We have the usual gas signal—an empty shell case—hanging in front of the bomb reserve shelter and at any sign of gas, the sentry beats the gong (or shell) with a bayonet or any handy chunk of iron.

January 12, 1916. Just before going to bed last night the mail arrived and on opening my share, I found a bundle of papers from the Breens containing packages and packages of Wrigley's Spearmint Chewing Gum. Is there no limit to these people's charity? I also discovered a packet of safety pins and six small crucifixes. When I opened the parcel everyone asked if I had one to spare. Kemball, a very solemn looking individual, hoped that they had been blessed by an Archbishop or somebody. Producing his wallet he took out a purple scapular carefully done up in tissue paper and proudly informed me that it had been blessed by a Bishop.

We have Stand To for half an hour before daybreak until half an hour after and [the same at dusk] and all ranks are dressed and equipped; the most favourable time for surprise attacks are these times.

Parade was the usual Rifle Inspection, Tube Helmet Drill and then I had my platoon man the parapets of the water-filled ditch that some joker called the "Fort." It is to this fort that they go when we are shelled.

At 4:35 this evening, just after the Stand To Parade, a great burst of rifle and machine gun fire started down on our right where some Guard Regiment is on duty. Flares and red rockets went up and a most furious din was sustained. Then our artillery remembered what they are drawing money for and they got into the game, hammer and tongs. The hubbub died down as quickly as it started.

(Heard later that the Guards had opened a heavy rifle fire as though preliminary to an assault in hopes of getting [the Germans] to man the parapet; as soon as they thought the enemy's trenches were full of men the artillery opened up a severe fire on them.)

January 13, 1916. To-day I had the company at work on the forts trying to put them into shape. At 10:20, the farm 400 yards from here was heavily shelled and I had some job keeping the men at work, they were so interested in the little shell game. At 11:30 the guns turned their attention to A Company's billet and planted two over the barn before the inmates knew what the racket was all about. Two more were sent through the barn and everyone beat it for the dugouts and trenches. One sergeant received slight flesh wounds but everyone else enjoyed it.

There is no doubt now in my mind but that good food is responsible for the greater efficiency of some of us officers over the men. If the men had as good food and accommodation as their officers, they would prove more efficient. I never before realized what good living can do for a man.

PACKAGES FROM HOME

It is a very queer thing that my address should be unknown to you. I can only believe that you do not read these novelettes. In any case, I am putting it down *again*.

Address my letters to: *11 Bn Sherwood Foresters. B.E.F. France—* and *nothing else* or I am liable to arrest for giving information.

And do not send me any more rotten junk except what I especially ask for. I simply have to throw it away and somehow or other, you certainly have the faculty of thinking of the wrong thing! Imagine that tube of tooth paste, for instance. How do you imagine that could be packed so that the contents would not burst through the ends?

Write to the Breens *at once* and tell them to address Catholic Records to me, if they wish to, and *chuck them in the stove.* The sight of the Catholic Record makes me grow as purple as a sporting extra.

I do not want my diaries spread all over the country and *you must get them back at once. If anyone wants to read them I want to know who they are first.* If I thought that these books were allowed to fall into everybody's hands I would soon stop them.

Tell Frank {*brother*} that I did not receive a package from any Patriotic Graft Fund Society this Xmas and I am much obliged to them indeed. They have done me better than some others I know of. Whenever I think of that Murphy woman's Xmas gift, I feel like firing 10 rounds rapid toward London in the hope of at least one shot getting home; because I am NOT a destitute and hungry Tommy, to be charmed and delighted with a lump of soggy chocolate and a half dozen rotten bananas.

After this, send me what I ask for only—and to the address which I have given and none other. If you cannot do that, then don't write and I will do the same.

January 14, 1916. I took a working party of 30 men up to the trenches this morning. The communication trench is called V.C. Avenue, and no better name could be found. It is not a trench at all, but a low breastwork, no higher than my neck.

The country here is low and level, so dug-in trenches would soon fill with water and become untenable. The only alternative is to build them up high and leave it to Providence to screen from a cross or enfilade fire as there is no wall, but merely a parapet and any shells bursting in the rear are liable to cave it in and demolish some intelligent voters.

The KOYLI (King's Own Yorkshire Light Infantry) lost three sergeants in three days, and another sergeant was wounded. One who gave up his ghost, was a veteran of Mons. The other morning, while under the influence of vin blanc, he mounted the parapet with his rifle in his hand, and waved "washouts" to a sniper who had taken a dislike to him. After about six tries, the Hun brought home the bacon.

I was greatly amused by the A Company in the trench-fort that they occupied. As soon as they were safe from a shell, their heads would appear over the parapet, and they would wait patiently for coming events. When the whizzing from the oncoming shell was heard, they would cry "Here she comes" just like fans at a race track, and then all the heads would duck until the burst was heard when they would immediately bob up again. It is marvellous the number of shells which the enemy wastes to get one of our men, yet they do get them sometimes.

INTO THE TRENCHES

January 15, 1916. We relieve the KOYLI today starting at 5 p.m. We are taking up only what we can carry.

The trenches are muddy, and the trench boards so slimy and greasy that every few minutes you slip off up to your knees or even your waist in a mud hole. I'm taking rubber hip boots. I am carrying my kit on my back, same as the men; officers are supposed to carry their kit, but most send up their luggage and wear inside their pack an inflated rubber pillow which weighs about four ounces and looks like 40 pounds!

So far, this battalion of Sherwoods have lost only 20 or 25 men. A number today are going up for the first time.

January 20, 1916. Got into the trenches and relieved the KOYLI all right last Saturday. We shall relieve each other every four days in the trenches. It is up to both regiments to leave the trenches just as comfortable as they can for the incoming tenants.

The trenches are always changing, as after each rain (or even heavy bombardment) the dugouts cave in, parapets fall down and parados (rear walls) become but a memory. Sniper's holes, machine gun emplacements and bomb rifle emplacements have to be changed too, as the enemy finds their positions and makes things—uncomfortable.

All this means endless rebuilding and our men not only work while "in" but each day we get a working party from KOYLIs in the support billets at the Rutland Arms. (When the KOYLIs are in, we send them a working party each day.)

(The habit of [giving] the front line trenches names is being discontinued, as the "Hohenzollern Redoubt" signifies nothing to a person who does not know where it is; with the new system of numbering and lettering, any Staff Officer with a map can find his way without a retinue of local guides.)

In our lines, we have two mines with several saps. These miners are an awful nuisance. They are continually bringing up sacks of mud and have immense piles behind their mines; some bags are in the path, squashed flat and horribly slimy. Work parties come and go, day and night, singing and talking loud enough to waken people in Potsdam. They are an undisciplined crew.

But for the last couple of days the Miners spoke in whispers, and had sandbag pads on their feet: they were running into the German saps: they were not sure whether the Bosches were below or above them, but they could hear them quite plainly and might break through into their position at any moment. At the saphead, bayonet men waited in readiness and the miners were armed with knives, hatchets and revolvers as they worked.

I took two men with me one night, and patrolled out in front of our lines, about 80 yards in front of the German wire. Our object was to examine the nature of the ground for cover to a raiding party (ours or theirs) but we were seen and one of their machine guns enfiladed us. We took cover in a river bed until they had exhausted themselves and wasted two or three Verey lights, after which we returned over our parapets. Later the C.O. sent his compliments.

In front of us is the River Lais, a small stream and quite low just now.

The ground in front of the German wire is flat and swampy. At intervals lie the bodies of British soldiers. I ran across seven or eight bodies: one or two (most likely officers, as they carried no packs) are covered with a thin layer of mud from head to foot. The majority are lying face down with full packs.

The caps, which I picked up, bore no regimental marks, and I did not look at the shoulder straps. I believe it was the custom for the assaulting troops to remove all badges so that the enemy would not know what Regiments were on their front. The clothing was rotting away as were also the bodies. In fact, many had no heads and in crawling behind a small hummock you found bones cracking beneath you: these bones proved to be the legs of a body and the hummock was, in fact, the pack.

German Artillery have been very active here, but confine themselves to demolishing support billets, shelling dumps, communication trenches, roads and artillery duels. Very little fire is played on our trenches by the big guns. A Company was the last to be relieved last night and I was in charge of the traffic at the far end of V.C. Avenue and so did not leave until 8:45 p.m., when everyone else had cleared out.

Our trench is (as usual) in a very sharp salient and an experienced German with a handy little machine gun used to delight in firing at our backs or at our parapet at unexpected intervals all night. He was particularly venomous at the trench end of VC Avenue, and he kept sand spurting from the bags and ripped the woodwork shamefully.

I came back across country to the main road and it was as well that I did, for at 9 sharp the Guards Brigade on our right, assisted by many of our guns, opened a terrific fire on the Hun parapet and the Bosche was not slow to reply. The air was alive with whistling bullets and bursting shrapnel. When I reached the road I found that they were playing the machine gun on it, sweeping from side to side to keep reinforcements from coming up. The night was made as bright as day by dozens of flares, and the bullets were like whips cracking. At Two Tree Farm, they were coming in so low that I was obliged to crawl into a ditch until our demonstration concluded with a final salvo of artillery. The enemy must have been badly scared for they kept Verey lights going all night, and their machine guns played the ground at intervals.

Did not arrive back at the Rutland Arms until 10 when everything was quiet.

It was quite a relief to take my clothes off and sleep in my valise once more (though we are liable to be called into the support trenches at any minute).

January 22, 1916. In the trenches. A Company, KOYLI messroom: a dirty little low shack, filled with smoke which oozes through a gap in the sandbags; the floor is a green, smelly sediment which was pumped from one of the mine shafts and enters the sandbag huts.

This hut (and better than most) is about eight by fourteen feet, and barely room to stand upright. The table is two planks resting on a double row of sandbags; for a bench, a single plank; the stove is a biscuit box punched full of holes and resting on bricks. The door is an ancient mail sack so muddy that a stiff wind fails to shift it. Rats and mice live here—and never are relieved.

FIRING A MINE

As we were coming along the front line at 7:45 a.m., a sentry halted us with the information that our mine was to be fired at 9. It was thought that the German sap, close to our line, might contain a bursting charge, and that our parapet or even trench might be blown in.

I went up to get a good view of the fireworks. At 9 sharp a dull rumble signalled the exploding of the mine, and earth rose up like a mushroom to a height of about 40 ft and slowly sank down again. There was so little noise (and it was all over in a few seconds), that men in the trenches nearby did not realize what had happened.

Not a shot was fired by either side and no movement was visible in their lines. This was strange as, when a mine is detonated, both sides usually open a heavy attack on the crater to prevent it from being occupied.

Soon after 10, the miners (who had been waiting to dash into the enemy's gallery, should one be disclosed) left the line. They looked very tired, as for three days they had expected to be blown to pieces.

We should have seven officers in our company, but we are now only three, and always on the go. We have been shelled every single day in our support billets so it is a relief to get into the firing line where they cannot use high explosives on us.

Four men were killed at Weathercock Farm yesterday, and eight wounded. Captain Brennan was blown into a ditch and now he is a nervous wreck, and will be sent to the hospital shortly.

We are shelled at all hours of the day, and the Ghost house is beginning to look really battered, but only one sergeant has been wounded and another received a severe shock when a wall fell on him. Luckily the enemy rarely shell at night because the flash of the guns gives their position away. (By counting the seconds between the flash and the sound of the gun, the distance can be roughly figured.)

Nothing seems to satisfy Martin lately but I believe it is nerves as he was only in the trenches for about a week in all before this. Every time he hears a shell coming, the most agonized expression comes on his face, and he watches me carefully to see if I, with my little more experience, consider it safe.

When we were in here last, I spent a lot of time in reconnoitring the disused trenches in our rear, and discovered trench stores in good condition. Taking two small parties, I managed to salvage trench boards, sheet iron, petrol tins, shovels, picks, bully beef and 5000 rounds of small arms ammunition. There remain other supplies going to ruin, but why would anyone go after them when they can get new stores?

January 23, 1916. Our Long Tom battery up the road has made itself so obnoxious to our friends over the line, that they (and we too, of course) have been shelled all day with very little respite.

A motor lorry, loaded with troops, came rolling slowly and majestically up the road and, in spite of our warnings, on through the firebeaten zone. When they got to the centre, several sappers decided to walk, so the lorry stopped while they dismounted and continued on foot. Their foolishness will be the death of them some of these days.

January 27, 1916. Going in last Sunday, we lost Lieut. Melville, our bomber. Seven others were wounded—the result of speaking too loudly and talking too much. They were heard in the German lines and shelled with whizz-bangs.

IN FRONT OF THE LINE

Monday night I took a patrol out to measure (for the information of the Engineers, Miners and Communiqué) the crater caused by that mine explosion on Saturday. I found it to be 63' diameter; 18' deep; 47 yards from our parapet and about 80 yards from the German wire—it is difficult to count out paces when you are crawling flat on the ground! A line of empty knife rests runs direct from our wire to the Hun's. I found this an excellent cover and guide up to the Bosche trenches. The only drawback to this route are the bodies which lie up close to it, but even these make concealment more possible. I think that this summer will see the absolute decay of these dead soldiers. I accidently put my foot through one on Monday night when patrolling.

The Mining Officers were astonished at the size of the crater. They now think that they have blown up an enemy's charge as well, and possibly croaked a few dozen "Gott mitt Uns." Let us hope so, anyhow.

Tuesday night I conducted another party of tourists out over the ground again. Half of my crush had never been out in front of a parapet before so look to me as a guide. Lieut. Kay of the Mining Staff confirmed my report and returned to his mine, but the rest of us lay out in front of the crater. Shortly before 11, I took them scouting across "No Man's Land" to listen for enemy patrols, working parties, snipers or listening posts, any of which are liable to be outside their wire at any time. A machine gun swept the crater so we lay tight and listened to the bullets humming overhead. (My main reason for taking them out was to give them confidence and teach them what to do between the lines. The Huns use as many as 50 men at a time on patrol and I would like to get our men used to working in groups so that we could handle one of those German patrols.)

Five minutes after we got back, the Huns opened fire with whizz-bangs, rifles and machine guns. Verey lights were sent up in dozens. Evidently they had caught sight of us and thought we were about to attack. Our men immediately poured back a rapid fire, the Yorks & Lancs on our left got into the game, C took it up and soon the Guards down on our right were blazing away—so our little patrol was responsible for a big demonstration.

Before we could stop our men, they got rid of nearly 3000 rounds of ammunition. The waste was all up in No. 1, left without Officers for a few minutes, and the men were enjoying themselves thoroughly, crying out, as they pushed a new clip into their rifles "Here's another for you, Fritz—and I hope you like it!"

However I think the Huns had the wind up all right as they swept our wire with machine gun fire all night and put several trench mortar shells in the crater. Our artillery was slow to reply due to poor communication, as the message requesting support has to pass through the hands of several Staffs. If our artillery had only opened up when the German parapet was lined with men....

We were so ashamed of the ammunition which our men threw away in useless fire that night, that I sneaked back to our old trenches the following morning and salvaged three more boxes of ammunition and that about covered what the men had shot off.

RELIEVING TROOPS

It is a picturesque sight when troops move in and out of the trenches at night. They march in single file without the usual grousing of the happy British soldier, each man fully loaded down; some wear Bomber's helmets which look like soup basins. Many wear fur jackets, like Robinson Crusoes. Odd men are additionally laden with wooden boxes containing periscopes, dixies, sniperscopes and other odds and ends made necessary by the present methods of warfare. The rear of each company is brought up by two stretcher bearers. The scene, thrilling the first time, soon becomes as humdrum as an English shopkeeper taking down his shutters on a Monday morning.

A Company was the last to leave and I led with No. 4 Platoon, taking a safe shortcut across the main road. Battalion HQ "Spy Farm," heavily shelled and set on fire in the morning, was still smouldering. From the trenches we had witnessed that bombardment and were surprised that not a single casualty resulted. All that was lost was a little equipment of the hundred odd men who occupied the place.

In answer to Bill's question, the stories told in the newspapers and illustrated with photographs taken "in the trenches" are not fakes; the only thing is that the Editor forgot to mention that the trenches were in England or alternative trenches 40 miles behind the firing line.

I believe that the French permit films to be taken of their troops, but no moving picture men are allowed to come near us out here.

No civilians are allowed in our trenches—except Premier Borden, Sam Hughes and other "highbrows" who would not be able to tell a trench from a deck of cards and therefore could do no harm if, later on, they told all they knew!

Speaking of civilians, brings to mind some oddities of this war which I may not have mentioned before. In Festubert during the battle, an old woman, the only occupant of the village, used to come to the door of her ruined house with a burning lamp in her hand and peer into the night to see what was going on and then disappear again indoors.

At Givenchy, outside the entrance to the communication trenches, I met an old dame peddling oranges, cakes, etc. The racket was awful, but she did not seem to notice.

Farmers work their fields with stray bullets flying about them— and well inside artillery range, often a mile or more in front of our guns.

Our artillerymen have a habit of firing over the cottages in front of their position. After a few rounds, the gunners drop in for coffee, then return to the guns.

January 28, 1916. Rue de Quesnoy. I stopped in to pay my respects to "Pa" Gaskell and the "Liverpool Irishman" Trayner. Trayner

(Q.M. of the Battalion) had lot to say about the burning of Spy Farm in which our #2 Platoon lost a lot of kit. When Trayner looked over the list, he swore that #2 must have spent all night throwing clothing and equipment into the fire and that we were a miserable set of Rob-dogs! (Privately, I might admit that some old shortages were included in the list.)

8:10 p.m. I am Orderly Officer again to-day but enjoy the work. While passing a party of Middlesex to-day, armed with picks and shovels, I overheard one of them moan "Six days shalt thou labour, and on the Seventh thou shalt rest—*I don't think.*" He had my sympathy, although I had to laugh.

Certainly these men have given up a lot to come out here. It was a sense of duty that brought them up to the colours at the first rush, and their home ties are more to them than any appeal which military life might have.

They earned good money at their trades in Nottinghamshire and Derbyshire and the separation allowance for their families is a mere trifle. These men are only paid a shilling a day and some allow their families half or even three quarters of this, so that they get only from six to twelve cents.

In their letters they sometimes ask for a few fags, soap or razor blades. Often, when they have requested some trifling gift, they apologize and hope their friends will not be put to too much expense.

The Officers are treated too well, and the men not well enough. (I have had a taste of both and I should know.) I heard one Captain say that he never ever told his men anything directly, but told the sergeant and let him deal with the "ignorant beggars who could not understand what was said by an educated man."

January 31, 1916. Thursday our old Battalion HQ "Weathercock Farm" met with a sad accident. All that is left of that once handsome farm building could be carried away in a hat.

Just got back at 2:30 p.m. in time to say "au revoir" to Martin who is going to hospital. Martin had a small cut when we were last in the trenches and washing in water from the River Lais has poisoned his blood; his face has broken out into a very bad rash. The river flows from the German lines through ours, and it is suspected that the Germans have poisoned it so it is used for washing only and not drinking. This trick is not at all beneath our gallant enemy—no unsportsmanlike trick is. Their snipers used explosive cartridges, as we can tell from the whizz of the bullet which is different from the clean whistle of a fair shot.

DISCIPLINE

...I have just finished censoring the mail and quote you a sample.

"*Well, I have not recieved that parcil from Uncle Arther yett and you still think it is coming yet. I bet it is coming yet and you still says he is sending you one but I say he is still sending well I think that he is not sending one at all now. It is a long time in coming any way I am still thinking that he is not going to send it at all but I am still thinking that it is on the way.*"

At first I suspected a clever code giving our position, area, number of troops, etc. away, but then I saw that our Kirkman was the author. This Kirkman is a dream. At present he is paying for the loss of a rifle and bayonet valued at about $40. He is paying by labour (at the rate of 24¢ per day) and in a few more months will be free from debt. If the War lasts long enough he may yet save enough money to buy a suit of civilian clothes at the end of it.

It is an *outrage* the way these men are soaked for loss of clothing and equipment. In the Canadian Cavalry, any of us who were short of anything simply went to the QMS and got it. Here if a man requests new boots or a shirt, they want to see the old ones and make up their minds whether the unfortunate blighter should get new ones free or have to pay. Many men are paying for articles lost, stolen or destroyed which the Canadians would just throw away.

Discipline is strict and men are given stiff sentences for trivial matters. Some in this company have several years in a military prison with hard labour hanging over their heads. After the war they will be sent to a quiet country home with a view through barred windows.

One chap, Bird, is undergoing Field Punishment which means without pay; his meals are cold water & bread. Not too much bread, either. This morning he was brought on the charge of "Losing by neglect his greatcoat and bayonet" and sentenced to another stretch, including one or two hours per day chained to a cart wheel. He was originally sentenced to be shot for his many offences but punishment was reduced to three or four years hard labour at the close of the war. That is why some soldiers hope for a long war.

February 2, 1916. I heard a man say, just before being marched to the baths "What's the use of my getting a bath, Sergeant? My socks are an inch thick with dirt." Sgt Connaughton turned and, furious, shook his fist under the unfortunate private's nose and bellowed "All right for you! Just bring me those socks after tea, and I'll wash them for you!!" Connaughton, a mild, inoffensive-looking man, is a regular demon with his men, and can get more out of them than a blood sucker.

NEW TRENCHES

February 3, 1916. Very cold to-day and we go up to a new line of trenches to relieve the 2nd Battalion Devons while they take over our billets here. Archer went up with an advance party this morning and No. 2 Platoon is to occupy Jay Post; the remainder in the firing line.

Some Tynesides, just over, are sending officers and NCOs to us to learn the routine of trenches, art of taking over, listening patrols, etc. RGA gunners have been spinning horrible yarns of life in the trenches. "Putting the wind up them" is an old game which is always impressive to a man just out from home

February 3, 1916. midnight. The enemy killed two men of this company already. One was shot in the Listening Post and Booth was shot as he stood on Watch. He only returned from leave in England yesterday, and leaves a wife and several children.

February 8, 1916. Fleurbaix. Came out of trenches last night and am now billeted in this town. The House with the Golden Pheasants is the title our home goes by and they are still in the back garden, looked after by the caretakers. This house was one of the best houses in Fleurbaix and makes a comfortable billet for those who are easily satisfied.

February 11, 1916. We left the trenches Monday night and my platoon had a real scare. We came out by Wye Farm, and were supposed to take #12 Emergency Road, but I found that a machine gun had swept the road beautifully so I continued on. Every 100 yards or so, the gun would open up on us and everyone would throw himself down and wait till the music had ceased. The stretcher bearers in rear were much handicapped by the long stretcher they carried as, every time they threw themselves down, it fell on them and banged their heads. When we got on the main road, we fairly dashed along until out of range and the men were nearly all in.

Tuesday last, I took a working party up to Wye Farm and we dug a deep ditch to drain off the water from the reserve trench and moat surrounding Wye Farm into the River Lais.

Wednesday, I took up a party to work in the Wells Farm salient. We were shelled heavily and our HQ lost a chimney and a few more windows. When we left, the shells were passing over us, bound for Fleurbaix so we came out by #12 Emergency Road and started for Elbow Farm—but the shells arrived first and started demolishing Elbow Farm, so we turned toward Wye Farm. By this time, the Huns started walloping Wye Farm, so we shifted our route toward Smiths Villas; we passed just in time to escape being hit by shrapnel breaking over it; we continued toward Limit Post and, 500 yards from there, we once more lay down alongside the road until the shells had given up. After that, we continued quietly to the billets.

Yesterday Martin returned from hospital. We were sorry, as Martin is very trying in his *in*-capacity of Acting Captain and tells us how important he is, and how insignificant everyone else is. Martin is not yet all right and may have to go to the hospital again. The next time I hope it will be nothing trivial. He gets on our nerves.

February 15, 1916. In my dugout 6 p.m. Sunday and Monday were wildly exciting days. B Company lost four killed and a number wounded, & we had one killed and three wounded on Sunday. On Monday, the Tynesides had a Major and several men killed or wounded.

The scene of festivities was the Wells Farm salient, the Chord Line, Abbott's Lane, Jay Post and our left flank. The cause of the rejoicing was a heavy bombardment by the enemy's guns on this part of the line and for hours we were covered with dense clouds of green, purple, orange and black smoke from all kinds of guns. The majority were High Explosive, intended to demolish the breastworks.

B Company absolutely lost their nerve and Maitland begged the

Battalion CO to send another company to relieve him and let B come to a quieter part of the line.

I got into trouble with Hudson, Brigadier General of this outfit, through my ignorance of Military Etiquette which demands that you say that everything is Jake, whether it is or not. When old Hudson came along this morning he asked me if everything was satisfactory and I replied that if the engineers would lay down more re-vetting frames we would get along faster. The old duffer turned on me like a lion and started to bawl me out for criticising another corps; he was so mad that he went down the line and called every officer all the disagreeable names he could think of.

COMING OUT AND IN

February 16. Limit Post (10 min. from Golden Pheasant House) 6:30 p.m. We came out of the trenches last night without any difficulty. Cpl. Mallatrat reported that he had come across a suspicious looking officer wearing RAMC badges and claiming to belong to the RGA; so I went and marched the RGA Medical Officer (for that is what he was) down the road and had him identified by the officers of his battery. Leslie Halford, OC of D Company was arrested in his own trenches by one of the Tyneside Irish and marched along with a bayonet a few inches from his backbone until one of his corporals got him free.

A German deserter crossed "No Man's Land," crept under our wire and over the parapet into a bay occupied by the Y&L. When the sentry saw the spiked helmet, he thought it was one of his pals, and called out "Hello, Mike. Where did you get that hat?" and the reply was "I haf coom to gif mine self oop!"

Very cold to-night with a drizzling rain.

February 17, 1916. We are so busy that I am unable to write as fully as I would like to, and my composition is decidedly falling off.

February 18, 1916. Manistee and Maitland had dinner with us to-night.... We have been reminiscing about the Tyneside Scotch & Irish. Where A and B joins on the Boutillerie line, an angle is formed with a bay and fire trench on each side. When the Tynesides occupied it, they seemed to get their sense of direction twisted and in each of these bays, the sentries were busy for quite a while in a wild endeavour to shoot each other. Fortunately neither sentry was a marksman.

The Germans are sending back some French prisoners with the welcome information that they can no longer feed them. It sounds fishy, but Trayner swears he met some of the returned prisoners in Sailly and held parley with them.

Cold and stiff gale blowing to-night. We are in for bad weather now.

February 19, 1916. 1:30 p.m. We are being supplied with steel helmets and all now must wear gum hip boots while in the trenches. The men present quite a different picture to the one painters and artists are so fond of: sentries now wear gas helmets rolled up on their heads with their helmet on top.

February 20, 1916. Trenches. We are very short of men now; only about a half a company & so can only man a limited number of bays; but we have enough sentries if they keep their eyes and ears open.

We came in without any trouble last night by way of Abbott's Lane and the Chord Line or London Wall. The Line was in fearful condition: half the trench boards were afloat in a foot of water and the rest out of sight in the mud. We were mud to the knees before we got through. The enemy snipers and machine guns were fairly quiet and only twice did we have to lie flat and wait for the racket overhead to cease.

One point in Abbott's Lane is very dangerous, where the trolley line crosses the trench; at this point, we have to walk fifteen yards in the open before getting down in the lane again. Luckily the Huns have not spotted that point yet and machine guns seldom play on it.

The trolleys I speak of are wooden tram lines laid down from the Dump where rations, etc. are unloaded from the Battalion transport to a point as near as possible to the firing line. The cars are like the trucks used in factories and are pushed along the rails by several men. The Germans, of course, started the idea and are supposed to have some excellent ration trolley lines down.

One point, just opposite to our present position, has a trolley with two branches at the foot running off to left and right. At times the Hun can be distinctly heard pushing his freight cars along the line. This trolley line is so well known that on our trench maps it is called Clapham Junction.

February 21, 1916. 1:30 a.m. I came on watch just an hour and a half ago and have another hour and a half to do before turning in once more.

Last night I had early watch; to-night, the middle one and to-morrow the last one. Sentries in the bays put up periscopes as soon as it gets light, but at night they look over the parapet without a glass, and only about half as many sentries are used during the day. Stand To originally meant that all ranks stood to arms from an hour before sunrise until an hour after; from an hour before dusk until an hour afterwards. The habit changed in the trenches to about fifteen minutes before and after.

After this, the section gathers for the Rum and Ration issue, supervised by an officer.

3:35 a.m. It is very quiet and some of B's sentries and their friends opposite, have been exchanging remarks in a loud tone of voice. The language from both sides is never used even by the most depraved writers, so I will not deface these pages, but I must say that these Germans swear very well—very well indeed.

NIGHT RAIDS

Feb. 22, 1916. I had the watch last night and intended to go out with Harrison and Ward at midnight to bomb the enemy's Listening Post opposite to our own, whose position we had thoroughly reconnoitred.

Brittan had never been on patrol before, so he left with Sgt Connaughton and four men at 11:15. They were merely to creep out in front and back again—more to instruct Brittan in the gentle art of stalking than anything else. It was not intended that they should stay past twelve as the moon comes out after midnight and patrolling ceases to be very safe.

Brittan's party proceeded with such *extreme* caution that it took them until 12:30 to return to our sally port, and by then the moon was out. They had only gone about 200 yards!

I was quite put out as it kept us waiting about until the Hun could observe movement on the ground in front. However, we decided to leave anyway. On their report that no hostile patrols were heard, we decided to make a speedy journey to the selected position which was on the edge of a ditch about 3' wide and 3' deep, with a row of stunted willows close to the stream on the German side. Our intention was to come up on the left of the Listening Post, about fifteen yards from it and throw the bombs from there.

Harrison and Ward carried four Mills Bombs each; I had bombs in my pouch. The revolver, of course, I had slung around my neck but I carried it in my hand when we got 30 yards from the German wire entanglements.

Before leaving, I instructed our sentries to fire an occasional shot high over the German parapet; moreover, as soon as they heard the explosion of the grenades, they and our machine guns were to open up a rapid fire on the enemy's parapet to keep the Hun's heads down and so cover our retirement

We left about 12:40 and crossed to our position. The little stream, bordered by stumpy willows, is closer to the enemy's parapet at one end than at the other; by a miscalculation, easily made in misty moonlight, we advanced to a very narrow edge of it, about 25 yards (I thought) from the enemy parapet and we lay tight to the ground while I tried to perceive against the black shadow thrown by the breastworks the exact location of the Listening Post which was screened by rushes that looked like rusted barb wire.

After creeping along to the right for a short distance, I was obliged to return and confess that I could not see it. Since we were so close to the parapet, we thought we might as well hurl the bombs inside at two places, one a bay with sentries (as frequent flashes came from it) and another spot where we could distinctly hear a man breaking kindling to keep a brazier going, no doubt.

I drew one of my bombs in readiness and told them to withdraw their pins and prepare to throw, when Harrison stopped me to ask what was that noise close by in the shadow of the parapet. One quick look was enough. I whispered back "Why, it is the Listening Post" and immediately Hun sentries opened rapid fire upon us lying fifteen yards away in bright moonlight.

The ground in front was ripped with bullets and the trees received their share also, as sparks flew from them. While still lying close to the ground I managed to throw my bomb, but failed to hear it go off and merely had the pleasure of hearing other sentries join in the general din with their rifles.

Evidently both sentries had called up their "waiting men" to participate in the fun, as two rifles on each side of the Post did excellent work in cutting the air directly over my head and all about me. (I use the word "me" advisedly as the two bombers disappeared so quickly that I almost wondered if they had ever existed. It was now a case of every man for himself.)

Then I commenced retiring, slowly drawing my body over the ground as I knew that I must get back into the hollows afforded by the folds of ground before they sent up flares, during the flight of which they could finish me in a most leisurely manner.

For some reason, possibly they were too excited, flares were not sent up until I put about 35 yards between the Listening Post and myself. When they did send them up, rifles cracked right merrily but they did not spot me; neither were their machine guns turned loose to sweep the ground with their terrible fire—and believe me, a boa constrictor is an amiable pet in comparison to a machine gun with its muzzle pointed toward you!

When the flares did go up, I lay close to the ground and simulated the appearance of a tuft of grass, not daring to blink while several flares fell so close to me that I could have touched them with my hand. All the time, I was wondering what had become of Harrison and Ward, both good, game boys, and I felt that if anything happened to them I would immediately organize a rescue party to bring them in.

As soon as there came a lull in the flares, I wriggled backwards, until I felt safe enough to turn and pad another fifty yards on my hands and knees. A hundred yards from our wire, I arose and ran, stooping, to our wire works, crossed this, then our burrow pit before the Parapet—and entered our Sally Port again.

My men had not returned, so I set out to search for them. Near the centre I lay in a shell hole and looked over the ground, when long, low whistles from our sentries signalled that they had arrived safely at our Listening Post.

These two also had had their little adventure: they had crawled rapidly to a ditch and fallen into about five feet of water. This ditch, at right angles to our lines, runs straight out to the stream in front of the German Listening Post. So they walked back all the way with only their noses showing above the water but they were thankful to get away with nothing more than a thoroughly wet suit of clothing.

March 4, 1916. Elbow Post. We left the trenches last Thursday night. The Huns had discovered a weak place in our parapet after they saw us at work building it up, and they kept up a steady sniping, yet we succeeded with the loss of only one man: a sapper attached to us for to help us carry on the remodelling of the trench. It was the first morning he had ever been in and an explosive bullet hit him in the head so hard that part of his head was blown 20'. (We had another sapper sent to us the following day.)

The night before we left I took Uttley, the Bombing Sergeant and Harrison, the wire man. There had been a very heavy frost and the ground was quite decent for our purpose, which was to bomb the enemy's Listening Post. It was just light enough to enable us to cross quickly and, after selecting a shell hole to which we could retire when the Huns opened fire on us, we moved forward to within 25 yards of the enemy's Listening Post. Just then, we heard some moving about and the sounds of voices as though the post was being relieved.

We stood up and Uttley threw three Mills Hand Grenades as I pulled the pins and passed them to him. Two fell within the post and the last one burst just over it. We got some Germans this time, and no mistake, as we heard them cry out and curse and only one rifle opened up on us from the post, instead of two or four.

However, their compatriots turned eight or 10 rifles and two machine guns on us, besides sending up innumerable flares. We got away with our usual good luck although the bullets whizzed about our ears and tore up the ground about us.

I was carrying my revolver by the cylinder and close to my hip as I crawled in. I felt one bullet strike the ground so close that it gave me a slight jar; when I got back I found that one shot had smashed the handle of my revolver tearing the steel frame apart. Another bullet, evidently a ricochet, tore a hole through my tunic pocket and penetrated a pocket book and some letters.

At our rendezvous near our wire, I found Uttley and Harrison excited and jubilant over our successful little raid. They said if we waited for a half an hour we might demolish the Bosche stretcher bearers who would have to come out and bring in the dead or dying; so we went back and had the machine gun trained on the spot where we expected they would come out.

The company at the parapet had seen the display. Since then, I have received all sorts of congratulatory remarks and there is talk of us being mentioned in despatches. General Gordon seems to have entirely overlooked a run-in we once had, and now thinks that I show signs of human intelligence for he greets me cheerfully, even jovially, while he passes by my seniors with a snap and a snarl.

We had a difficult time in getting out of the trenches Thursday as nearly all the road routes were swept by bullets, but we did get out with only one casualty. Our communication route seems to become more difficult each time we go up.

March 5, 1916. Father Bell was waiting for me at Elbow Farm when I returned from Mares Nest and he wanted to know what kept me from church and other personal matters. He is very well liked and calls on us every time we come out of the trenches. To-day he complimented me on my bomb-raiding exploits, which seem to be common talk among the Brigade. After tea, I walked up the road with him and he made me make my Confession and promise to go to Communion on my very next time out provided I could get away. Anyhow, he gave me absolution!

THE DIARY KID

Ray Johnson, a happy go lucky joker whom everyone would like to see left at the base, so they tell me, paid us a call this afternoon. He was in great humour but I am afraid that he will soon go to pieces with the strenuous trench life. We had not been chatting very long, before he turned to me and said "You are an American, aren't you?" Americans and Canadians are popular among the English here and I am always called in mess "The Diary Kid;" "Klondike;" etc.

BACK IN THE LINE

6 March, 1916. 9 p.m. In the trenches. I think the Huns have discovered not only that we relieve here every four days, but also the exact days on which we do relieve for, on those nights, the road behind the firing line is diligently swept with machine guns, rifle batteries and rifles. Anyhow, they kept us ducking and diving tonight, but we managed to arrive without a casualty.

March 7, 1916. 3 a.m. A new addition to our trench stores is a dummy figure of a soldier known as "Pte. Marmaduke, #1,000,001." He is a most awful-looking figure, and has a ghastly head of wood with the weirdest kind of paint on its face. D Company gave Marmaduke an excellent character saying that he had been used on sentry go for 10 hours at a stretch without a murmur from him; he *never* complains about the food, sauces his NCO or leaves the trench without permission. (But—he is useless for work parties.)

The Hun has a new invention: an elephant gun or a gun taking a very large cartridge with a steel coated projectile about 3" long and provided with telescopic sights. In those parts of the line where the parapet was thought to be weak, it is trained on a spot about a foot below the sentry's fixed periscope. These bullets have been known to penetrate three sandbags and kill the sentry.

Ash Wednesday. 1916. It is very cold. Nothing exciting to-night, merely the usual sniping of the sleepy sentry who can see nothing but merely presses the trigger at intervals to keep awake. We fired some rifle grenades from one of our bays and had the satisfaction of seeing them drop on the enemy's parapet where they made quite a roar, if nothing else.

Early to-night, Martin and his Jam Tin Artillery Brigade (the Trench Mortar Battery) held a demonstration assisted by a herd of machine guns. The enemy made no response and we think that there was nobody home.

2 a.m. Just discovered a sentry asleep and on investigation found that he had been on ever since 6:30 last night. This is a serious mistake for someone, as a sentry is supposed to do only one hour as "waiting man" (which means sitting on the fire step beside the sentry and taking his place should some lucky shot spoil the sentry's appearance); then he becomes the sentry; after another hour he gets two hours rest. Asleep on sentry while on active service is punishable with death, but this man will get off with a few weeks F.P.#1, as he is not altogether to blame.

March 13, 1916. Yesterday and today have been beautiful Spring days, with some early flowers out.

We were relieved late on Friday night by Capt. Pyeman and his crew of KOYLIs. I brought most of the company out by way of Abbott's Lane communication trench which has now reached the dignity of a river and we were all soaked to the knees (except for those who managed to fall off the trench boards into one of the many mudholes lining the route, and these luckless stumblers were pulled out half drowned).

TIME OFF

Sunday I took half the company up to the baths at Sailly. Walked up again and attended the Cinema Show and entertainment at the Sailly Empire. The building can seat 200 men and 40 officers, besides the Divisional orchestra. The brick walls are hung with coloured posters from Blood 'n Thunder Films; it looks very like Ed Glasgow's old prize ring parlour above our store. They tell me the house is packed every day. (A few Hun shells accurately placed would do no end of damage when a show is on.)

Charlie Chaplin and the Keystone Company are great favourites, but John Bunny was received in solemn silence. A film depicting the marvellous exploits of a New York detective in rounding up a bunch of Black Hand Bowery terrorists was received with howls of merriment by men who are accustomed to daily dangers worse than the New York detective ever dreamt of.

Had lunch with Pyeman, who is becoming very energetic. He has arranged a Trench Mortar Evening for tonight. The mortars are 60 pound batteries with a 500 yard range and a sweep of twenty degrees. It takes thirteen-and-a-half seconds for one shell to go that far and by that time Fritz is clearing his bays, charging his whizz-bangs and getting ready for some retaliation.

The last time this battery did some strafing was at the Bois Grenier when two struck the enemy parapet making holes eight by sixteen feet. In one of these holes the sociable Hun hung up a board bearing the inscription "A jolly good shot!"—and then bombarded us for three solid hours, inflicting over 50 casualties.

March 14, 1916. 11:30 a.m. This is as fine a morning as you would ever have in summer. Everything is drying up, so that soon we can expect to see the roads deep in dust instead of mud. The birds are chirping; a field battery behind us is banging away right merrily; two hostile airplanes have just been driven off by machine guns, and now antiaircraft sections from the RHA are adding to the din.

Today I walked to Port à Clous farm, for Mass in a barn. The altar was a portable affair carried in a suitcase and set up on a packing box. The men were very devout, and sang several hymns from "The Soldiers' Prayer Book." Just before Mass, Fr. Doe glared about and I feared that I was in for a Regimental Bawl-Out, but everything turned out all right.

We go up to the trenches again tonight. The addition of a half company of the Royal Sussex Regiment should enable us to get a great deal of work done this time.

{John Teahan was wounded on his way into the trenches that night.}

On Sick Leave

DUCHESS OF WESTMINSTER'S HOSPITAL

St Patricks Day. 1916. *Bed #4, Ward C, Duchess of Westminster Hospital, Paris Place.* Well, now I'll tell you how it happened. You see, it was like this. I led my platoon, intending to go by Wye Farm; however some genius had blocked that road, so we were obliged to take "Gunners Walk" which everyone else uses, but I have always suspected that the enemy have discovered our days of relief, for it is always bullet-swept when we go in or come out.

Davenport, our sniper, was the leading man and, as he seemed very tired, I relieved him of his cumbersome sniperscope. I carried it on my left shoulder so that it more or less protected the left side of my head. About halfway up the trench (which was only waist high) I felt a smashing blow on the cheek such as a boxer might deliver. I did not know exactly where the bullet (or whatever it was) hit me as, while my face was covered with blood, no particular part of me seemed more stunned than another. The flash of fire which I saw just as the bullet struck, made me suppose that a misguided sky-rocket had turned the trick.

As soon as I had got my bearings and allayed the excitement among the men behind me, I ordered them to go on, with the exception of one man (whom I left lying in the trench to warn other relieving parties that they were in a Danger Zone) and Brown whom I took to escort me back to the Dressing Station at Wye Farm.

There I was attended by our own Dr. Macdonald. Mac said the bullet had gone in near my right temple and come out through my left cheek, and that I would be on leave for a month. (I knew better, though I did not argue.)

Capt. Fyldes and Major Burnell were astonished that I would get hit three quarters of a mile from enemy lines after so many narrow escapes.

The CO ordered a special ambulance car. I was on a stretcher, and have been a "lying" case ever since. I was taken to Nouveau Monde, innoculated against tetanus and put in another ambulance. I awoke as they were carrying me into a hospital which looked like a school. I was visited here by a couple of the 9th J&Ls who had been shrapnelled in Fleurbaix a few days before, and are hobbling about with their legs full of fragments.

About 2 p.m. the hospital was evacuated of as many patients as could be moved. I was taken to the train where I was given the middle bunk in a finely appointed stretcher car.

A young machine gunner who had been out only about five weeks, began to tell how awful the other rotten corps were (not even omitting his own). He ran foul of a couple of Bantam Brigade *{men below normal standard}* officers when he told us of how the Bantams used to tear down the crosses over the graves to keep their braziers burning. The Bantam Brigade officers picked up his remarks and made him eat them in regard to their own battalions, so then he put the blame on the Bantam Highland Light Infantry which seemed to satisfy everyone!

It was dark when we were unloaded at Etaples, warmly wrapped in blankets for the ride to the Duchess of Westminster's—formerly the Paris Place Casino. It is for officers only. Patients sent here are considered lucky.

The beds by the walls, equipped with thin iron railings about eight feet high, can be screened off into separate compartments. So I feel quite privileged in a box stall with a music cabinet on either side, a bentwood chair, and five pillows. I have a fine view of the main drive and pass many a pleasant hour watching hearses galloping up and down the drive, and long processions of mourners.

March 18, 1916. I was X-rayed in five different positions, and I have a slight skull fracture, a blood clot on the eye and tiny fragments of steel distributed about without any regard to my beauty.

We are quite a sociable party. No. 3, a Major from the unfortunate 11th Royal Sussex, got shelled in the Fleurbaix billets. The Hon. N. Lytton, son of the Duke of something or other, lies with a chunk of shrapnel in his leg. He was in the trenches only once, and then for just a few hours.

On #5 reposes the doughty champion from the Bantam Brigade, Lieut. Joplings, 19th Durham Light Infantry. Next to him is the piano: half dozen were left here when the Casino furniture was removed to make a hospital. The Duchess comes in every day and drops a pleasant word or two to some of the old stagers. Yesterday, she insisted on propping me up with pillows stolen off the Honourable's cot.

March 19, 1916. About 400 men and 27 officers arrived at Etaples on the hospital train last night; seven officers were admitted here; the rest were bundled off for the boat train.

We get all the magazines and books we wish for and daily papers are brought around every morning by aged French newsboys—too old to join the army, anyhow.

Col. Martin, #2 dugout, kindly sends me over Punch's, and Maj. Lytton has a small library near his bed so we never want for reading matter. As for food, there is really too much of it and all cooked by a chef (commandeered with the Casino). I can have anything I want and unlimited drinks at lunch and dinner but they will not let me get out of bed. I feel perfectly all right now except that my right eye is as black as ink which makes the Gloucesterman insist that I was in an estaminet escapade.

March 20, 1916. The Duchess called to-day. She is a tall girl, about 24, not bad looking and dressed something between a nurse and a vaudeville actress. She finds the hospital a fearful strain on her nerves and repeatedly declares that it is an *awful war*—but one of the orderlies tells me that she spends three months in Blightie and four months in Switzerland. When it all begins to pall, she dashes back here for a rest.

She was describing some German prisoners the other day: "One was such an awful, awful brute. He lay on his face the whole time and grunted at everybody."—and went on to explain that the big bully's captors (evidently Canadians) had been in such a hurry to turn their prisoner over and get back to the firing line that the Bosche received no less than 47 bayonet punctures in his rear. And now, Gentle Reader, I ask you: would you sing Songs of Praise and Hope if you had a back like a pin cushion—or would you lie on your face and grunt?

However, the Duchess' patronage and aid in obtaining contributions is joyfully received.

HOSPITAL SHIP

March 21, 1916. On Belgian Hospital ship Ostende in the harbour of Calais. Left Le Toquet this morning still on a stretcher, in pyjamas, muffler, sleeping cap with a tag around my neck like a prize winning porker. I was labelled "COT" Class A, which means A1 Treatment, and I am getting it too. Three of us ("3 Lying Officers from the Duchess of Westminster's"), were taken to Etaples and put on the Hospital train for Calais. I believe that the whole hospital is to be cleared to either England or the base so that the hospital will be ready for the annual Spring Bargain Rush.

We arrived on the boat in time for an excellent tea. Our ward on the main deck (likely the former music room) is small but very fine. Our beds have crib sides and swinging trays so that we each have a dining table. Opposite is Lieut. Manson, a Varsity graduate, and we have been talking Toronto and the Canadian Contingent for the last couple of hours. Manson spotted me for a Canuck when he first heard me say "ground."

March 22nd, 1916. We leave at noon. The Belgian Captain takes no chance on bad seas in which his men are apt to overlook floating mines; he crosses very slowly, sometimes taking three hours for the run.

The work is light and consists of lying in bed and chatting with those of your neighbours who feel anyway fit.

2 p.m. Just off Dover. Through my window I can see the chalk cliffs. Poor Manson says he hopes his next journey will bring the Citadel of Quebec into view. I am afraid he will not be much more use out here as he cannot support his head, having lost control of the nerves connecting head and neck.

Some officers are discussing what hospitals they prefer: we have a choice if we wish to insist upon it. I do not care but have been marked for an Eye Specialists' Hospital.

QUEEN ALEXANDRA'S MILITARY HOSPITAL, LONDON

8:30 p.m. "K" Ward. After a first class lunch, we seven cot cases were carried onto the platform of the Dover Station, laid in a neat row and left there until our train came in. Munn (brother of the 2nd Bn N&D Adj.) wanted to know if we were left there to encourage recruiting or was it to put heart into new drafts going over. He compared us to a lot of hares drawn up after a day's hunt to be photographed and so prove the prowess of the hunters and he suggested someone dressed as the Kaiser standing behind us, leaning on a machine gun.

At Charing Cross the M.O. asked where we wished to go but, as soon as he found out, he made excuses and sent the victim someplace else. However, the QAM has a good name and I have not been in it long enough to raise a holler—yet.

The ward is very good, and dinner was fine: linen and cutlery, bearing King George's monogram, the whole set on a small table which could be wheeled to the cot. Good beds with a table and reading lamp; several easy chairs are about. Nothing is left undone that could give the inmates a thoroughly enjoyable time.

A heavy mist hung over everything as we were driven through the streets. They make sailing almost impossible as lookouts cannot distinguish floating mines until they are on top of them. The mines are painted like the water and marked on top to imitate the foam on the curl of a wave. Manson tells me that in Wireless HQ they are continually picking up calls for help and he believes that more than one ship has gone down unreported. Even fishing smacks and other small boats disappear.

March 23, 1916. Have been looking at my name in the Roll of Honour—the morning edition of the Daily Mail's Casualty list.

9:35 a.m. Just finished an overwhelming breakfast and I feel quite happy now. Really it is not such a bad old world after all.

My nurse says that I will likely be allowed to wander around by the weekend. Freedom of the City, as it were.

I do not know anyone here yet, but a Captain in my room amuses me very much. He got smashed up near Ypres and is lame, deaf, blind in one eye and apparently a little childish. He looks as though he had been bombed, starved, shelled and dragged through a hedge backwards.

10 a.m. I like the Senior Doctor very much. (I heard since that he is a Jaw Specialist.) After looking at my dope sheet he exclaimed dramatically "What—Sherwood Foresters!" and then, to the Junior, "My worst cases come from the Sherwood Foresters." After this, he had me bite each of his fingers and seemed disappointed. He told me reproachfully of one of his last Sherwood victims, a beautiful case: he had had all his lower jaw blown off and they had to stand him on his head to feed him. When I timidly suggested that the X-Rays might show something, he brightened up at once. I feel sure that the good man would love to replace my jaw with a bundle of laths and an old circular saw.

11:30 a.m. The ward looks very cheerful, with rugs and small tables standing about, each with a vase of flowers or a brass jardiniere of palms, ferns, etc. The attendants continually try to force fruit, candy, books, & magazines upon us. No sooner are you rid of one, than another makes an appearance and, like beggars, if you accept anything off of one, the rest become peeved.

On Leave in Canada & England

{One book is missing here.}

OTTAWA AND MONTREAL

Frank *{brother}* and I spent the day in Ottawa. I was cooked in my heavy tunic and my reception in Ottawa did not make me any cooler. I went to interview Col. Biggar, Director of Transportation, to try to get the Canadian Government to refund a $3.10 War Tax on my passage back from England. The sum, in itself, was nothing (not even repayment of the trip to Ottawa) but [I wanted] to see just how far the Canadian Militia Department would go in their slighting treatment of returned soldiers and especially Imperial Officers.

Col. Biggar (I may be in error regarding the first vowel) received me with a snarl like a wildcat and a face blue with passion—or maybe heat. I presented my papers and he snarled "You are an Imperial now. You will have to see *them* about your claims. This is Canada and you have to pay your tax like anyone else." Then he added "We paid your way over to France, didn't we?" and when I admitted it, he yelled *"Well, what more do you want?"*

And he said if I wished I might present the claim to the Minister of Finance and see what he would do with it. He ignored my salute both on entering and leaving and acted in every way like an Officer and Gentleman.

When leaving Ottawa we noticed some girls who were booked on the same boat. Frank saw them first and he hooked me in the ribs so sharply with his elbow that I had to go into the Smoker and get a drink!

On arrival in Montreal, we were herded about the platform while an over-worked commissioner of the Allied Line tried to round up the Ottawa ladies' party and luggage. Frank and I, the only men in the bus, made ourselves useful at the dock, unloading luggage and carrying it to the gangplank where we were to show our tickets and passports.

You cannot imagine my astonishment when I was told that a War Office Passport authorizing my return to duty would not allow me to board the boat: I must have photographs and Letters of Identification. After a hot argument, the Clerk told me that if I got two photos, the Letters of Identification would be made out at the dock, and so I turned wearily away to get "mugged" and "Bertillioned" *{method of identifying criminals}* to satisfy Canadian Immigration.

Just then an old lady, whose grips I had carried, stepped up and pressed a quarter into my hand, saying "Take that, my good man." I protested, but she kept insisting that I buy myself and my friend a glass of beer. It was with difficulty that I escaped a tip. (If it had not been so funny I would have felt dejected at having been taken for a porter while wearing the uniform of an Imperial Officer.)

Even the faithful but wilted dog, Frank, smiled—but not for long. I insisted on walking all the way to Bleury and St. Catherine Streets as we were told that it was a ten minute stroll. It was really no walk at all, as the hill was not very steep; the bag, which Frank carried, was not heavy (very heavy, that is) and it did not start to rain until we were nearly halfway through our mile and four furlongs sprint, yet Frank grouched and whined and cursed the entire distance. However, we got the photos and later, an excellent supper at the Windsor Hotel.

About 11 we drove back and the Immigration Officer, without any question, filled out an L.O.D., affixed my photos and had me sign it. There was no identification at all—just ridiculous red tape.

We met another victim of the system there: Capt. J. March, 1st Newfoundland Regt: he ran about Montreal half the night trying to get his photos and had to change to mufti, but I looked so mad that nobody tried to prevent me from wearing a uniform. (I heard later that other officers were obliged to buy or borrow overalls, and sneak aboard like workmen.) It made no difference what you wore on board, but no officers other than Canadians are allowed to go aboard in uniform.

BACK IN LONDON

July 30, 1916. Grand Hotel, Trafalgar Square, London. I took a double room at the Strand Palace for March and myself.

Out of March's battalion only two officers are left at the front and, with luck, the survivors may make up half a battalion by the time they all get out of the hospital. I met several hobbling in and out of the hotel and their tales of the charge at Beaumont were blood-curdling. The men charged at 9:30 *in broad daylight* and not one reached the German trenches.

Called on Colonel Watson in St. Thomas's Hospital, Lambeth Embankment. He described how his battalion got theirs and showed me letters from Brig. Gordon, and General Hudson congratulating the 11th on their gallant work. The 9th KOYLI lost every officer, and the 11th Sherwoods only saved three or four. Harris and Russel were blown to pieces and the battalion is now but a handful.

Later I called on Manistee (B Co.) in a new Hospital—16 Bruton Street, Berkeley Square. Manistee has a fractured leg and a splintered arm but expects to be around again by next Xmas. He seems cheerful and says he is glad to be out of it for a while.

Ray Johnson crawled up a tree to watch the effect of our shells on the enemy lines and a sniper shot him so now he eats his meals from the mantel piece, but expects to be back in another month.

Wyatt and "Tiny" Martin got cushy wounds; Wyatt was shot through the cheeks and Martin only lost a foot or leg or something. It seems that the 9th KOYLI rushed first and got across, but the 11th S.F. were dished by crossfire in No Man's Land and never got near the enemy. No-one seems to be at all clear how it happened and I only got rambling stories.

One officer said the charge by two Australian Divisions was over a two-mile frontage before Armentieres. They captured 149 Germans and a few guns, but lost over 2000 men. Newspapers headlines read *"Successful raid by Australians—149 Germans and many machine guns captured"* when, in reality, the attack was a grim failure.

It is hard to know what to believe these days as the papers publish so many "Grim Fairy Tales;" the only thing you can go by is the casualty lists and they are so heavy that you rarely find the names of NCOs and men; the list seems to be taken up by officers. This morning's Times shows 580 casualties to officers, 143 killed and 50 "missing," which is as good as dead—if not worse. Losses in the ranks numbered 5,770.

After March left, I went down to Surrey. I spent a week there loafing and sleeping, but it got too monotonous, so I am back at the

Grand.

July 31, 1916. Saturday night I saw Fred Lukes of Amherstberg, formerly a sergeant in the 1st Hussars, and now a lieutenant in the CMRs. Lukes has been in Folkestone ever since his arrival four months ago. He says that the base is absolutely packed with Canadian officers; when their units were split up into drafts for the front, they were left behind. A lot are in mufti and only appear on parade often enough to make sure that they are not overlooked on paydays.

Their behaviour is disgraceful, and all England is talking of it. In France I heard many tales of them, more yarns in Surrey and now Lukes and Miss Maxwell who just returned from Folkestone not only corroborate the stories, but add to them. The Metropole is nightly the scene of drunken orgies by Canadian officers who stop ladies in the street and invite them up as their guests. Miss Maxwell said she was stopped repeatedly by officers who tried to strike up a conversation.

One officer married a barmaid in one of the Folkestone hotels. Another married a girl he met two weeks before; on their honeymoon, he gave her such a severe beating that the police were called in.

I met an agent on the Grampian for a Montreal jewellery firm who specialize in the manufacture of military badges. Henderson, years ago, was a Major in the militia. He described graft in Canadian depots in England. (He, of course, is making money on the war too.) Henderson thought it was quite a joke to see Canadian officers drawing Staff pay in England for doing nothing. He said that a friend in Shorncliffe offered him a Staff appointment with his old rank. The rate, including allowances, runs anywhere from 10-30 dollars per day for these thieves whose lives have never been endangered for one second. And they have no intentions of going to the front, not only because of the danger or the high pay they get for *not* fighting, but also because many have been assured of Permanent Army appointments in Canada after the war.

The graft does not stop with the officers. The Canadian Pay and Record offices employ enough men to run two such departments. They hold Staff NCO appointments, and draw down more pay and allowances than junior Officers in the trenches. Some, but not many, of these men have been to the front and, of these, the majority are private soldiers who average twenty dollars per week, more than most ever earned in their lives.

10 p.m. Every night about this time, the Red Cross train arrives at Charing Cross and crowds gather on the Strand to see the wounded taken off in ambulances. The crowd neither jeer nor cheer but some of the more kindhearted say "Poor old things" etc, and a few weep.

A week ago Saturday we dropped in at Hyde Park in time to see the Women War Workers' parade. They were a tough-looking lot, and I wonder if their menfolks are not pleased to be safe in France in comfortable trenches! All sorts of occupations were represented: window cleaners, chauffeurs, munitions workers, farmhands, farmers, dustmen, etc. I think laurels for "hardest-looking" should fall on the engine cleaners, wipers and oilers, who are employed by the railways—as fine a looking lot of ladies as ever cracked a safe.

August 3, 1916. Received an immortal poem by that crazy old bat Angela Breen. I laughed myself into hysterics over it, and I hope to give her lots of material to carry on the great work with. Also a letter from Mattie {*a cousin*}. This had been opened by a Censor somewhere. I hope the advice (about sacred medals and the value of attending Mass) did him good. Not even a tip on the races to gladden the poor old censor's heart.

August 5, 1916. Grand Hotel. About 8 p.m., S-Lt Cunningham and I went to Hyde Park. We visited all the little meetings going on—Atheists, Anti-Vivisectionists; Christian Knowledge Proof Society; Temperance; Freethinkers; Salvation Army and two or three others whose reasoning, argument or aim we could not comprehend in spite of our endeavours.

The Temperance people had a wonderfully successful evening and their joy knew no bounds when a drunken soldier staggered up to the orator's stand and solemnly affixed name to the Pledge.

Two sharp featured women held individual Indignation Meetings about unknown subjects, and discussed in learned language such interesting and local topics as "The Whyness of the What" and "The Whereness of the When."

This afternoon I took Miss McLaughlin bus riding. At London Bridge we saw some of Lord Derby's drafted men. Some looked a good deal older than 40. The young men shaped up better and I wondered why they had not been sent over long ago: I suppose that they are a family's only support—but they have to go at last.

August 6th, 1916. In nearly all the restaurants and tea shops the waiters are foreigners -Swiss, Italians, French, Belgians etc. They are exempt from duty where the Englishmen have got to serve with the colours. I suppose "They also serve who only stand and wait"—but it seems unfair while our people are dying to defend their country. Friendly Aliens are now being registered and the scenes about a Registration Depot are as good as a show. The penalty is 200 pounds and Imprisonment, so the aliens are registering, all right!

August 7, 1916. Many hospitals have sprung up: vacant houses fitted up for convalescing officers, though some are very makeshift.

August 8, 1916. I had to report twice at the War Office, today. I went in at 11 a.m. and was told to come back to be given particulars about my case. So at 5 p.m., I was Johnny at the Rat-hole, and they slipped me the dope that I was under Southern Command, and I was to wire *them* to see who has my papers.

August 9, 1916. 12 Noon. In an L&SW Coach, Waterloo Station. Received instructions this morning to report to Southern Command, Salisbury. I followed the good old plan of approaching the Railway Transportation Officer with an immense bundle of official looking papers; throwing them on his desk and demanding a return warrant. He raised a few shrieks of agony but I lied manfully, swore the War Office had sent me and he fell for it.

7 p.m. County Hotel, Salisbury Wilts. The Chief Medical Officer finds that my papers are either at Tidworth or Reading, but I am to stay and report at 2.

August 10, 1916. This hotel is very old-fashioned—like Inns in Dickens' time. The waiters are elderly men wearing dress suits with unpolished brass buttons and cloth of a respectable dark green tinge, with that reverent stoop which only years of practise in leaning over guests and giving advice can bring. Dinner was only marred by the rude stares of a fishy-eyed Major no doubt wondering what my Green Cross meant. I was on the point of going over and smashing him on the nose, when guessing my intentions, he shifted his eyes onto the table.

5:45 p.m. Prince of Wales Hotel, Ludgershall, Wilts. At 2 p.m. I again visited the M.O. Southern Command and was told that my Medical Board had been arranged for Friday, in Tidworth Military Hospital and that the ceremony is booked for 12.

Tidworth has no hotel so there was nothing for me to do but

come back up the line to Ludgershall.

August 11, 1916. Tidworth, Salisbury Plain. 2:10 p.m. There are 40,000 Australians training here (and they tell me that this is only an item compared to other troops in England) so I guess old England will ride safely through the storm.

I had to wait here until noon before they would consent to "board" me, and then I visited the eye specialist. Next I took my papers before the Board. They said I could have my papers marked "General Service."

They asked if I would like more leave—perhaps a week. But I said that I had had quite enough, so they gave me a warrant up to Cannock Chase where I suppose I join the first lot of drafts. I think from the way that I have been treated that my military services must have received a boost from Col. Watson. He told me when I saw him in hospital that the Brigadier (the same one that bawled me out for a quarter of an hour on a previous occasion) had said "Be sure you get Teahan back again. He is worth six of some of these other fellows!" and I call that some boost—especially from Brigadier Gordon!

August 12, 1916. 11:45 a.m. Euston Station. On the way back to the hotel last night, I was stopped in Piccadilly Circus by two privates from the Royal Montreal Regiment, 14th Batt. Both wore wound stripes, told pathetic stories and wanted the price of a flop. I fell for it, but wished later that I had called a Military Policeman and given them free lodgings!

It is disgraceful for Canadian soldiers to beg on the streets, and the whole Canadian Force gets a bad name.

Received a letter from the War Office this morning, advising me that my medical board would take place at Reading, at noon—*yesterday.*

"LIGHT DUTIES" IN STAFFORDSHIRE

9:15 Officers Mess. 14th Btn Brocton Camp, Staffs. I hoofed it up to camp here and saw the Assistant Adjutant. I am quartered with Lt. Vivian, who seems to be a pretty decent fellow.

Capt. Brennan (who was with us in France and got shell-shocked during the bombardment of Weathercock House) is the only one here whom I know.

They tell me Col. Brittan is a stickler for military etiquette. He will not recognize a salute from an officer without gloves, and all that sort of thing.

August 13, 1916. This is quiet country, and rather pretty—hilly and covered with gorse and heather. We are in huts about two miles from Milford and Brocton Station. 13th Batt. N&D are about three quarters of a mile from here. Behind us across the valley are the Leicesters, Lancashire Fusiliers and the West Riding.

August 14, 1916. I am attached to Brennan's Company, and he told me that I would have as little to do as he could manage. Our total strength is 93, all conscripts in different stages of training.

This morning, we had five officers & seven men on parade, the rest being on lectures or fatigues. Three officers are going to the RFC and that leaves Brennan and me on our own.

Brennan's term of "light duties" expires next month, and although he says he will be glad to be sent to the 11th, I do not think that he is eager to go out for another winter and—I doubt he will make it.

QM Houlihan also took down all the claims that I could think of (not much) and added all that he thought of (quite a lot) and we cooked up an expense bill against the War Office to the tune of ten guineas! He wanted to claim for my return expenses from Windsor, Ontario, but I did not have the nerve!

August 15, 1916. 12:20 p.m. Orderly Room. We have to put on slacks for dinner here and if you are caught on the parade ground or the road without gloves you are liable to a severe reprimand.

All the officers here profess to be bored to death, but they prefer it to being bored to death in France. Another 11th S.F. officer, Clarke, has arrived. He was knocked out a quarter of an hour before the charge on July 1st, and is unable to tell us much of the affair.

August 17, 1916. The men now receive only 8-12 weeks training before being shoved across to France; sometimes drafts, with but five or six weeks instruction, are also shipped along. We have no company drills: men are divided (depending upon their time of arrival) and are known as "3 Weeks Class," "5 Weeks Class," etc.! Every few weeks, the Senior Class march to the station along with drafts from other battalions and, two days later, are in the Division Base in France.

I saw 40 of them led off this morning after a small ceremony in which the martyrs were handed a few bars of chocolate, a pipe, tobacco and cigarettes—quite ample recompense for the hot time ahead of them. Our consumptive Fife & Drum Band led them to the station, joyfully tooting "When the Boys Come Home," and the draft trailed along, with sick-looking grins on their faces. Really, it was laughable.

What we are going to do when this lot go, I do not know. Brennan says he cannot see anything for it but to raise the age limit and force in the foreigners. Nottingham and Derbyshire Counties seem pretty well cleaned out, and we figure the war will last at least another year.

August 18, 1916. The brigade, consisting of seven reserve battalions (9th Lincolns, 14th West Yorkshires, 13th Lancashires, 13th Sherwoods, 14th Sherwoods, 14th Manchesters and 11th West Riding) are holding a route march today. They are very short of men: all seven would hardly make one battalion.

Commencing next month, they will do away altogether with reserve battalions for each regiment and, instead, have one or two reserve battalions of mixed regiments. Many officers and NCOs now used for training will immediately be sent on service.

August 19, 1916. Sunday is like one long 12th July celebration. Fife and drum bands leading church parades keep passing on their way to the Church huts, and from all quarters come the rumble of kettledrums and the shrill of fifes; each tries to drown out the bands of the next battalion. One regiment has a brass band; the rest have to get along with fife & drum racket-makers. A little music is all right, but these fellows overdo it.

Our band used to practice all day till neighbouring huts put in a complaint. Then they went down the hill near the Sewage Plant until the Colonel had a deputation of labourers call on him and said the noise interfered with their work!

Applications keep coming in, requesting that certain soldiers be allowed leave to bring in the harvest where the only help to be had at present are boys, women and old men.

August 22, 1916. Alcock and I took a company for Night Operations. It was a farce. Alcock tried to make it interesting for the NCOs by letting them lead the column using my Prismatic Compass but, as no-one knew how to work it, the scheme fizzled.

August 25th, 1916. Last night a Competition Concert was given for the men of the Battalion. The contestants were divided into classes: Sentimental songs; Humorous songs; Recitations; Dancing and the Best Imitation of Charlie Chaplin. The Sentimental songs were humorous; the Humorous songs were pathetic. A drummer named Whipple sang a ballad about a "Birdie with a Broken Wing," which would have brought down the house only we could hardly understand a word. An ancient soldier with five ribbons on his breast then annoyed us with *"Lord Robert's Farewell Speech to the Officers and Men of the South African Field Force."*

We have a great time here with recruits who shirk at the Butts under the mistaken impression that if they never hit the target they will not be sent to France. (Some suggested that if they had a couple more months practice they might become more proficient.) When it is supposed that a man is firing off the target on purpose, an instructor takes his place, the man gets a record as a First Class Shot and off he goes in a hurry!

Just before a draft, some men parade before the doctor with imaginary ailments in the hope of being left behind. Doctor Telfer says that they have either consulted a medical man or read medical books; if they really had the symptoms they claim, they would only have about a week to live.

A man in A Company, charging sham trenches while carrying a full pack, attempted to simulate a faint, but two instructors dragged him to his feet and forced him over the jumps at the point of bayonets. At the last trench they tried to throw him across but they missed (whether intentionally or not I do not know) and he fell to the bottom like a sack of coal. He will leave with the next draft.

Often, now, a couple of odd recruits come in, and then we have a sergeant drilling a class of two men. The 14th Bn of West Ridings is being disbanded for lack of recruits; its officers and men are to be distributed among other battalions.

August 26th, 1916. County Conservative Club House. Stafford. After lunch, Brooke, Shaw, F.A. Pyle and I walked in here by way of Walton. During tea, our conversation turned on military matters and Colonel Brittan, Captain Frodsham, Ass't Adj. Ingram and Morgan came in for some very severe knocks. They are not fit to lead a parade of Boy Scouts and if any one of them was ordered out on Service he would have heart failure.

August 28th, 1916. The Lincolns sent a large draft off this morning and we have 80 leaving at midnight. We will soon be cleaned out of men. We have some old soldiers left, of course, but these men are not fit enough to stand the strain of trench warfare, so they are kept in readiness for Home Service or they may be drafted to some foreign station to relieve troops who are fit. It is honestly pathetic to see some of these old men bravely shouldering their packs and stepping out alongside quite young boys.

SHIPPING THE DRAFT

August 29, 1916. We had quite a little celebration last night when shipping our draft. A Company (from which all drafts are sent) was in a turmoil: the men had got well oiled in the Canteen and there was much singing, interspersed with loud yells. Sgt-Major Farnsworth was about driven crazy with them.

He had them out on the Parade Ground and, in numbering them off, some men could not—or would not—number correctly, so Farnsworth walked down the line tapping each man on the chest and bellowing his number. About half-way down, he would run into some privates who had stepped up to shake hands with a pal in the draft, and Farnsworth would get so mad that he would forget the count and have to start all over. The next time, he would be interrupted by some bibulous individual calling on everybody to give three cheers for the "Notts & Jocks." So Farnsworth put the Sergeant-Major's Curse on them and hoped that each and every one of them would get from the Germans what he himself would like to give them!

At 1 a.m., the Band fell in ahead and, to the air of "The Young May Moon," the draft started off, cheering madly, to begin their Great Adventure, followed by eight "waiting men." "Waiting men" are always sent along to fill up the places in a draft should any men desert on the way to the station which is on the other side of a Common where men could easily get away in the darkness. However, none of this crowd tried to do so, and the waiting men returned with the Band.

Our draft was followed by a very small party of our 13th Bn, who cheered lustily, if a trifle incoherently, for the "Old Stubborns" and close behind, were the 9th Lincolns' Band heading another draft and playing their "Lincolnshire Poacher." Across the valley we could see lights flashing in the Lancashire lines, and hear their bands playing the "Marseillaise" and "Until the Boys Come Home."

There were several weeping women about the roads who accompanied their husbands all the way to Milford & Brocton, but I must say that the women did not give way altogether here, nor cause any scenes at the stations either.

11:30 p.m. This morning we subs were put through a strenuous lesson in the old method of Bayonet Fighting by the Battalion Sgt-Major Instructor, who certainly knows his business and proved it with the Warwicks in this war. I was much amused by the businesslike way in which he went about his lectures. He illustrated, by means of an imaginary opponent, just how to stab him under the chin and make him remove his hat; how to break a man's neck with one blow or flatten his face with the brass butt of the Lee-Enfield. I particularly enjoyed his little masterpiece of a lecture on footwork: it was really thrilling when he showed us how, by kicking a man severely in the stomach, you could withdraw your bayonet point after it had gone through him; also, how to back-heel in the face a fallen opponent and otherwise pulverize your enemy.

September (?) 1916. I have been Acting Company Commander for the last couple of days. They told me this morning that Brennan was leaving us, but failed to say whether I would be made Company Commander or not. I know that my name is on the list to go out with the first draft and Active Service will I am sure suit me much better than messing about training camp, even as a Company Commander.

After tea, I got into mufti and went into Stafford with some of the boys. My mufti aroused a lot of comment and some laughter. The Adjutant merely grinned and advised me not to let the C.O. see me. Had dinner and returned after 11.

PAYING OFF THE BATTALION

Today is the last day of this Battalion—the 14th Reserve Sherwood Foresters, so all the companies were paid off this afternoon. This is the first time I have ever assisted in paying out the English soldiers at home. I was much surprised to see the small amount of pay they drew after bills for shoe and clothing repairs, haircutting, etc. had been deducted from their accounts. Most received three shillings (and some, only one) but all seemed to be well satisfied.

It would astonish you to see these men line up, wait their turn, approach the table, salute, receive their shilling, salute once more and walk away clutching their single coin. The humour of the thing is that for all we know some of these men have motor cars at home. In fact, among the last lot were a broker and an attorney

September 1, 1916. The concert last night was a great success and I enjoyed it much more than turns in the ordinary Music Hall; but then, I always did prefer soldiers' concerts and I have had more enjoyment out of a Cinema Show & Concert given in a ramshackle barn a few miles behind the trenches than I could get in an elaborate London production.

The surprise of the evening was Sgt Major Farnsworth in his "Comic Selections and Patter." A stout bull-necked man with a face like a grouchy potman, he looks like a typical Army Bully—the stamp of sergeant who enjoys himself most when bulldozing the men up and down the parade ground and "Blasting their eyes" at the top of his lungs while blue smoke and sulphurous flames leap from his mouth. He is the last person in the world I ever expected to hear singing comic songs. I never felt sure but that the next verse might not be a trifle worse than the one before, but he remembered that there were ladies present and saved some for the Wet Canteen later on.

September 5, 1916. Black Bay Hotel. Nottingham. Copestake, Clifford and I to proceed at once on 48 hours leave and hold ourselves in readiness to report to the M.L.O. at Folkestone.

2:40 p.m. Strand Palace Hotel, London. There seem to be a lot of soldiers about town and not so many in civvies as I saw in Nottingham where a great many men are in munitions factories. They are getting very strict all over the country now and police sometimes round up men not in uniform. Those who have not satisfactory papers are taken up until they can prove themselves or they are delivered over to tender-hearted drill sergeants in military training camps.

The medical examiners are as lax in their examination of recruits now as they were strict at the beginning of the war. Volunteers who were turned down two years ago, are snapped up. Now we have recruits with lung trouble, varicose veins and flat feet; they even take men with one glass eye! I expect that by Christmas, men between 41 and 45 will be called up. Next Spring, the British Army will mostly consist of cripples.

September 11, 1916. I am very much surprised at not having been told to report at Folkestone before this; I might just as well have stayed in Brocton and awaited orders. I wired the Adjutant of the 14th S.F this morning, and told him I was still here, in case they had forgotten my existence.

Yesterday at St Patrick's I was tapped for the usual double collection plus seat toll. The priest read out a pamphlet by Archbishop Bourne, which smote the Germans hip and thigh and called on Catholics throughout the world to assist in every possible manner the Allies in their war. At least one bishop has the nerve to call the Germans anti-Christians! If the Pope were not such a weak man he also would call upon the world's Catholics to help destroy the Huns.

September 12, 1916. My service kit is packed and ready right down to the necessary French coinage, and yet I hear never a word. (I suppose if I had only one shirt I would be ordered out of the country in an hour.)

I invested in a body shield and believe it will ensure me against shrapnel or bayonet wounds in the chest or back. I do not expect to get hit but it is just as well to go prepared, if only for the confidence it will give me.

September 13, 1916. Received a letter from the War Office this morning; I have been granted a wound gratuity of £104/3s./4d. This is not nearly what I was led to expect, but no doubt I will be allowed a pension at the close of the war. With the notification, they enclosed forms advising investment of at least part of the wound gratuities in government bonds.

EMBARKATION ORDERS

11 p.m. Received telegram: *"Report Assistant Embarkment Commandant Folkestone by 10 p.m. Saturday 16 inst. Train leaves Charing Cross 9:37 a.m. Please acknowledge. Adjutant 13th Batt. Training Reserve."*

September 14, 1916. In Hyde Park overlooking the Serpentine. Went to Cox's this morning to see about my gratuity and was told that I receive it in two instalments of which the £104/3s./4d was the first; another cheque will become due when the Tidworth Medical Brigades evidence is docketed. Then I can expect a pension which should not be a penny under 100 pounds per year.

The usual collection of wounded soldiers is now in the park. The Officers limp, hobble and drag themselves by in their own uniforms, but not so the poor Tommies. It is not bad enough for a Tommy to be wounded, but the hospital must needs advertise his misfortune by dressing him in a mis-fitting awkwardly-cut uniform with a white shirt and red necktie. The uniform is either a dirty grey flannel or a deep blue that fairly screams for vengeance at the red necktie. Men fastidious about their clothing in service or civil life, must feel their position very keenly, dressed up in this manner. The idea is, I believe, to mark them so that they cannot obtain liquor from any pub or through a kindhearted individual.

6:10 p.m. A Zeppelin was brought down in flames a few weeks ago. I believe that everyone in London saw it or the burst of flames that followed. All the picture shows have a film about it and photos are sold on the streets. It is amusing to see respectable-looking old ladies and gentlemen joyfully recount just how much of the affair they saw and gloat, when describing the wreckage containing the mangled bodies of the seventeen miserable Germans of the crew.

September 16, 1916. Folkestone, Queens Hotel. Met Clifford, Brooke, Rastall, Pettigrew, Copestake, Wheatley and Statham on the boat train platform. There were very few people there to say goodbye to their friends, and no cheers as we left.

Aboard S.S Victoria. Off the coast of France. Left Folkestone just an hour ago and had a fast and pleasant trip, like the Belle Isle ferry. We were guarded by destroyers and torpedo boats and a dirigible balloon, like a shark sailing in the air, went ahead nosing about for submarines and mines.

In France with the 16th Battalion

BOULOGNE TO CALAIS

September 17, 1916. On the Nord Railway en route for Calais. Arrived in Boulogne about 4:30, and had a long wait before we were instructed go to Calais.

September 18, 1916. "B" *lines. Sherwood Officers' Mess. 14th Infantry Brigade Depot. Calais* We did not leave Boulogne yesterday until nearly 1 p.m. The train went so slow that often the men got out and walked beside it; when they got too far ahead, they would sit down and wait for the Flyer. We frequently stopped while the engineer got up enough steam to blow his whistle at the next crossing.

Once here we reported to the Orderly Room. Copestake and I are down for the 16th. I am not anxious to leave the 11th and do not care for Copestake's company in any battalion. Copestake was gazetted 2nd Lieutenant nearly 21 months ago—and he knows less now than he did then. They must have had temporary madness when he was accepted.

I wrote Col. Watson last night, asking him to apply for me again and telling him of my being drafted to the 16th battalion. All Officers who were out to the front before were immediately drafted into companies here, while inexperienced Officers have to attend the "Bull Ring," which means a hard gruelling every morning in squad drill, rifle & bayonet exercise and musketry: work that is given the raw recruit—only the Officers are put through it rather rapidly.

I am in command of G Company—about 190 men but 75 are going up to the front tonight. We are in bell tents which leak like sieves, and last night it rained heavily as it has done all morning.

7:15 p.m. Earp and I went down into Calais to the "Chrystal" Palace cinema; other cinemas are run in estaminets in which you must buy drinks. The Chrystal features American films. It was odd to see these films produced with French reading matter; even the inevitable lost letter (which always furnishes the key to the plot) was in French.

September 19, 1916. There is great discussion here about the armoured land ships or "tanks" which are being used so successfully in the Somme. A few of the officers had heard of these machines but it was news to most of us.

6:30 p.m. Raining again and very cold. I have been sleeping all afternoon while the other fellows went through gas tests which turned all their brass buttons a dirty green. We have a piano in the anteroom, and four rattling good players among the officers, so I pass some time in there with magazines, chess and checkers.

8 p.m. The meals here are really rotten for an Officers Mess. We had corned beef stew, today. We are charged 2fr per day for our messing, and I believe someone is making a nice rakeoff on us.

Another large draft is leaving; a most miserable leavetaking as it is raining in torrents and they will be drenched before they arrive anywhere near the Calais depot.

September 20, 1916. Among the men I inspected today are a dozen young fellows among the draft being returned to England for temporary Home Service: they will be sent out again as soon as they turn nineteen. Some came over by falsifying their age and have seen heavy fighting in the Somme, but their people brought the matter up before the military authorities and have had the boys returned.

2 p.m. A rumour has just come in that the 2nd Battalion of Sherwood Foresters has been cut to pieces, and only one Officer and 32 men are left. So I expect the rest of us will move shortly. I hope so, for this wet camp is entirely too similar to Salisbury Plains.

September 21, 1916. My company was reduced by drafts to only 30 men, and 24 of those are going away tonight, so I am to be Commander in Chief of a half dozen.

September 22, 1916. 10 p.m. At each base depot 50 men who are physically unfit for active service are put to work burying the dead and looking after fortified positions. These jobs used to be given to men with motherless children but now they are being sent up to take their chances with the Bosches at close quarters. This is pretty hard lines. Some are really old and trench life will soon kill or cripple them, providing a bullet does not stop them first.

BRUTAL TRAINING

This morning I was in charge of a depot of drafts going to and from the "Bull Ring" where the men are given over to sergeant instructors who use them in a brutal manner. Pritchard went with me, and we were all set for a nice morning's rest, when the Instructor-Captain came up and ordered us to follow him for instruction in bombing.

First we threw dummy Mills until my back was near broken and then we threw live Mills. While we were busy at this, the men were at bayonet practice, running over obstacles, squad, musketry, physical drill and, cruellest of all—a long run, wearing gas helmets on their heads while carrying fixed bayonets and equipment in battle order.

I saw three men fall to the ground, absolutely exhausted. Two of these were yanked to their feet by NCOs but the third man, and an old man too, was dumped unceremoniously behind one of the trenches and there he lay face upwards. I took pity on him, and Pritchard and I went across, loosened his clothing and removed his equipment. I would have given his head some shade from the sun, but our Captain-Instructor called me away and gave me a severe checking off for being "soft-hearted" and also for "lack of discipline" for paying attention to a half dead man.

About noon, we subs were taken in hand by the gas experts, and given instruction in the new quick fitting of the gas helmets, and then run and marched about the grounds. After this, we were locked in a chamber with the thickest possible gas; then a dose of lachrymose gas; then another run about the camp with gas helmets on.

We finished at 2 p.m. with a March Past the C.O. It was a fearful ceremony, conducted through a double line of Sgt Instructors who barked at the men as they passed, criticising their step, method of carrying rifle and equipment, carriage and general appearance. Two platoons were sent back to repeat the performance and one was made to do it a third time.

Pritchard and I were quite fed up by the time we were allowed to march off, and we decided that we would not go back again if we could get out of it, especially as I was on the point of coming to blows with the Captain-Instructor.

September 23, 1916. Since taking over here, the Quartermaster has sent up to the line over 30,000 reinforcements, and now wants to go himself to see what has become of them all. I do not think that they will let him go, as he must be almost 60.

ZEPPELIN

About 11:15 I went to bed, and had hardly got into my valise when we heard the coughing of the Archibalds (anti-aircraft guns). We came to the entrance of the tent, and there in the sky with three searchlights on it was a Zeppelin—the first I have seen. It looked like a bar of silver, being the same colour as the moon, while the searchlights played on it suspended in the air and apparently motionless. It looked to be about eighteen inches long and four inches thick, with rounded ends and movements so slow that you were surprised at the end of five minutes or so to find that you had faced about and were looking in an entirely new direction while watching its manoeuvres.

A few preliminary shots were fired at it, and then the air was filled with blazing skyrockets; all of them fell far short. The Zeppelin was really moving very rapidly at about 5000 feet and seemed to be directly over our camp. Some of us thought we were in for a night of cross-country running to avoid being bombed; however it veered off, circled about us and headed for Calais, the sea and possibly for England.

MARCH TO THE CALAIS DOCKS

This morning at 5 o'clock my servant woke me and handed me a message detailing me to march a work party to the Base Supply Depot East Docks, Calais and report there at 7 a.m.

At 6:10 we started off. There was some trouble as to the location of this Depot: no-one seemed to have heard of it before. The Sergeant Major cursed them up and down, swore that they were not fit to leave their mothers, and then—admitted he did not know where it was, himself!

Another sergeant came along, and said he knew: it was "the place where the burned sandbags are." So we gaily started off to find the burned sandbags. (If the pile of sandbags which marked the site of the Depot should happen to be unburned I wondered where we would go next. It reminded me of Jason setting out to find the Golden Fleece, but anyhow it was not my funeral. I was in charge, it is true, but only in the capacity of a disinterested and even bored participant.)

After marching about two miles, we brought up at a canal bank near some RE stores and reliable witnesses that I had brought with me swore that the burned sandbags were or had been near that spot. I sent two NCOs to RE's Orderly Room to find the truth about the elusive B.S.D. and its pile of sandbags, and was informed that, while he knew nothing of sandbags, the Supply Depot was three miles away.

So off we set again and after much marching (which took us within half a mile of our starting point) we reached the West Docks, and then after more talk and more marching arrived here at 8:15. I turned the party over to the A.S.C., and have the rest of the day off. (At the moment, I am sitting near the bridge and have a fine view of Calais' congested harbour.)

(By the way, that pile of burned sandbags turned out to be a myth, for this depot is marked by huge piles of boxes bearing the well known Green Shamrock by which foodstuffs are marked.)

4.45 p.m. I fell in with a subaltern named Holland of the South Staffs, who also had a working party on the quay. After lunch we toured the sea front and saw several French torpedo boats and destroyers which lay alongside one of the docks. What I liked about them, next to the sloppy appearance of the vessels with the men's washing hanging all over the rigging, was the gypsy-like picturesqueness of the sailors. The dirtiest and grimiest of them were the N.C.O.s—possibly because they did all the work; the only Officer I saw wore clothes that might have been used as pyjamas in a stable.

We also saw about 30 German prisoners under a guard of four Frenchmen, being marched to the quays for to work. The French put them on all such jobs now, loading and unloading stores, repairing roads, etc. These men must have had good food to keep so fit. A few had the blue forage cap of the French soldier and one wore a Stetson "a la cowboy." The Lord knows where he got it but he looked a scream in it with his Hun uniform!

9:30 p.m. Left the docks at 6 p.m. and we took a short cut back to camp. The men sang joyfully on the first leg of our journey, but on the home stretch they fairly whooped it up and one of the favourites seemed to be "Michigan." This bothered me at first as I thought they might be trying to pull my leg.

September 24, 1916. This depot supplies drafts from the Sherwood Foresters for other battalions. Last night a party left for the line and I was surprised to see them wearing Warwickshire cap badges while they retained on their shoulders the familiar Notts & Derby badge.

It is rather hard lines on these old soldiers (who have come back wounded from the Battalion where they have friends) to get sent to a different Regiment. Sometimes a County's Regiment wins a fine name for its share in an action when its men came from a different county and Regiment. Several times during this war, the backbone of Battalions which won great honour were Sherwood Foresters drafted to fill the gaps.

{*End of manuscript.*}

FROM SHERWOOD FORESTERS' WAR DIARY

Thiepval. October 9, 1916.

There was no artillery preparation. ...In accordance with orders, the Battalion made an attack on the Schwaben Redoubt. ...The assault was carried out at 4:30 a.m., under cover of darkness. The assaulting waves had not gone more than half the distance across No Man's Land before enemy machine guns and rifle fire was opened. Our casualties were heavy, numbering thirteen officers. ...Other ranks 26 killed, 134 wounded and 64 missing.

[John Patrick Teahan was reported Missing in Action October 9, 1916. His body was never recovered.]

JOHN PATRICK TEAHAN was born in Southampton, Ontario, in 1887, the eldest of twelve children. His father moved the family to Windsor in 1906, where he opened a furniture store that John managed for him until the outbreak of war. John Teahan was a talented musician in great demand as a singer at weddings and concerts throughout Southern Ontario. He was also interested in sport —particularly horse racing—and became a well-known amateur boxer. He enlisted at Amherstburg in August of 1914, sailed to England in November of 1914 and died two years later at Thiepval, France, on 9 October 1916.

GRACE KEENAN PRINCE was born in Windsor, and has lived since then in Toronto, Nigeria, Jamaica and the Canary Islands. For most of that time, in addition to raising seven children, she has worked as a librarian, writer and editor. Her essays and stories have been published in a number of newspapers and periodicals, including the *Globe and Mail*, Montreal *Gazette* and *Queen's Quarterly*, and she has appeared on both the CBC and independent radio. She currently lives in Montreal.